How to Spell Chanukah

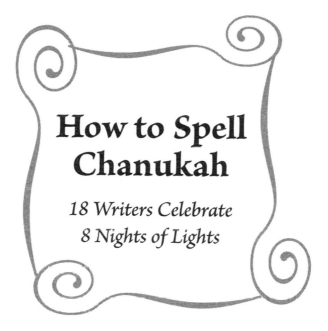

How to Spell Chanukah

18 Writers Celebrate
8 Nights of Lights

—— EDITED BY ——

EMILY FRANKLIN

ALGONQUIN BOOKS OF CHAPEL HILL   2007

Published by

ALGONQUIN BOOKS OF CHAPEL HILL

Post Office Box 2225

Chapel Hill, North Carolina 27515-2225

a division of

WORKMAN PUBLISHING

225 Varick Street

New York, New York 10014

Printed in the United States of America.

Published simultaneously in Canada by Thomas Allen & Son Limited.

Design by Anne Winslow.

Library of Congress Cataloging-in-Publication Data

How to spell Chanukah: 18 writers celebrate 8 nights of lights /

edited by Emily Franklin.

p. cm.

ISBN 978-1-56512-538-4

1. Hanukkah.   2. Jews — United States — Anecdotes.

I. Franklin, Emily.

BM695.H3H68 2007

296.4'35 — dc22   2007014207

10 9 8 7 6 5 4 3 2 1

First Edition

ACKNOWLEDGMENTS

Thanks to: Amy Gash, Faye Bender, Heather Swain, and Adam, who gives me a year-round festival of lights.

For my children

Contents

Introduction

....

~~Hanu~~ ~~Channuk~~ Chanukah

TWO YEARS AGO, THE SMOKE DETECTOR WENT ON OVERDRIVE IN THE MIDDLE OF MY LATKEFEST. REINFORCEMENTS (IN THE FORM OF HUSBAND, IN-LAWS, CHILDREN) WERE CALLED TO OPEN THE DOORS AND FAN THE AIR WITH PLACE MATS. I STOOD IN THE KITCHEN, GREASE STAINS ON MY PANTS AND SHIRT, SMOKE INFLAMING MY EYES, AND WONDERED WHAT THE HELL I WAS DOING.

After all, growing up had hardly been a plethora of potato pancakes. Chanukah came and went with only a few years of lighting the candles, but on December 24 my brothers and I piled into the car to head—stereotypically—to Grandma's house

....

(though hers was a brownstone in Boston, not a cute cabin in the woods). It wasn't that all Jewish traditions went amiss, but Chanukah, quiet and unassuming, got pushed aside, the wallflower of Jewish holidays. We had a menorah, but we also had stockings and a ten-foot tree complete with ornaments we'd made.

"Can you make cheese latkes this year?" my seven-year-old asks me at the market.

"Um, I could . . ." I answer, thinking back to the smoke-filled kitchen. The truth was that two years ago I'd gone a little overboard. Between my prior days as a chef and my desire to make Chanukah every bit as enticing for my children as Christmas had been to me, I'd spent hours grating. Not just regular potatoes for pancakes — think sweet-potato latkes, zucchini latkes, half regular – half sweet pancakes. "Maybe this year we'll just do a big batch of regular latkes. Okay?" I watch his face for disappointment.

He nods. "Sure. But we'll still have gelt, right?"

My turn to nod. The small mesh bags of plastic-tasting chocolate coins still make me happy. The kids look forward to it, and my husband and I laugh while listening to the Leevees' tune "Gelt Melts." (Favorite line: "If Goys can eat a chocolate bunny, why can't we eat chocolate money?") "We'll definitely have gelt."

"And charity night."

"Of course."

I thought I would miss the holiday time I had as a kid. What I know now, having watched the season morph from tree to menorah, and deciding with my husband to let go of Christmas and embrace the festival of lights, is that what matters to us — to the kids, to our family — is making the holiday our own. We have traditions: latkes, gelt, a night when one child chooses a charity for us to donate to and we skip gifts, rotating years for each member of the family to pick a cause. The kids decorate the dining room with Jewish stars, some crayon-colored, others coated with glue and sparkles. And when we light the candles, with all three of the kids (ages eight, six, three, and six months), there is magic in the room. Each night is a little different; each year is, too. Variations on a theme.

THE ESSAYS IN *How to Spell Chanukah* speak to the variety and the sameness of Chanukah. Ranging in tone from comedic to snarky, poignant to poetic, each contributor shares with us the meaning of Chanukah as they've experienced it. As many ways as there are to spell the holiday, so are there ways to enjoy, anticipate, loathe, and love the festival of lights.

This year I will be appreciating the small things — watching my children's faces when they sing the prayer over the candles, hearing my husband play from the sheet music I've bought him as a gift, tasting the oily crunch of biting into a latke, the pleasant combination of sour cream and applesauce, and the flicker of lights. I will enjoy the quiet that comes after we've tucked the kids — and each of the eight nights — away. And then, perhaps nibbling on a leftover pancake or trying — yet again — the plasticky gelt, I will curl up with a good book. May you enjoy doing the same.

Emily Franklin

How to Spell Chanukah

JOSHUA BRAFF

The Blue Team

As a ferociously reluctant yeshiva boy in the 1970s, I thought that Chanukah was without a doubt the most joyous time of the year. Unlike the four hundred and twelve other Jewish holidays that surround it on the Hebrew calendar, the festival of lights used to arrive like a life raft of optimism for any of us who felt Judaism had been crammed down our throats. And yes, of course, it, too, is a holiday that recalls an incident in which a mighty king decided that the Jews of the time where having too much luck or fun or prosperity. And yes, of course, this resulted in mass bloodshed throughout the streets of Judea. But unlike Yom Kippur and Rosh Hashanah, it was always made

clear that the story behind Chanukah held relatively little significance. And I always appreciated that. It was about a guy named
Judah Maccabaeus and his four brothers and how they rebelled
against King Antiochus because he ordered the chosen people
to reject God and all their Jewish customs. After three years of
gorging each other with spears and swords, the Maccabees won
the war and the Syrians were forced out of Judea, which would
become Israel. Judah and the boys reclaimed the Temple in Jerusalem and were granted a miracle of eight days of light from
only one day's worth of oil. The result of this miracle for me was
that my horrific school was closed for a week, a mountain of gift-
wrapped boxes formed in my living room, Rudolph and Santa
Claus were both on TV in Claymation form, and not once did
anyone tell me to fast. Even my Moroccan-born yeshiva teachers
were in good moods, showing us their tobacco-stained smiles
for the first time since Purim.

Each December when the Chanukah winter break arrived,
the principal, Rabbi Litsky, would hand us a gift as we got on the
bus that Friday. I called them "Chocolate Jews," but they were
Judah Maccabaeus – shaped candies wrapped in blue-and-white
tinfoil. When you bit Judah's head off, he was hollow inside and
you could wear him on your pinkie and lick him like a cocoa lol-
lipop. What a holiday! No pestilence, no slavery, no locusts, no
cattle disease or atonement. No synagogue, no guilt, no mortar,
and no real lesson to be absorbed and passed down to my Jew-

ish offspring. Thank God. Chanukah was merely the blue team in the color war against the mighty red team, Christmas. We were smaller and got way less press, but who could deny that eight days of presents was oh so much better than one? All that buildup they had with the chimney and the cookies and the sleigh bells ringing and it was over in a New York minute. But with all the obvious differences, I always thought the two holidays had quite a bit in common as well. Both were intended to be religious events but seemed less about God and more about the mall. Both had bearded men on their respective wrapping paper, both had just dynamite, knee-tapping songs written for them, and both were celebrations of truly brave Jews.

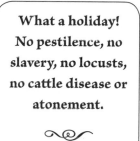

What a holiday! No pestilence, no slavery, no locusts, no cattle disease or atonement.

Chanukah in our house also meant it was time to bring out the papier-mâché replica of the Temple my mother made around the time I was born. I'll have to ask her what gave her the gumption to do this; she constructed a dollhouse, really, a miniature synagogue with a sanctuary and an arch with tiny Torahs and plastic Maccabees and little Hasidic men who came complete with tallises and long gray beards. I think the dome of the building was made of a Tupperware fruit bowl and the tan walls were cardboard, and I remember maroon carpeting and a bimah with pulpits. In hindsight, there was no greater way for me to shed my frustrations with the rituals of yeshiva life than to play with the Temple B'nai fruit bowl. I set up all the evil Syrians in battle formation, making them surround the synagogue with spears in hand. Then I removed the dome so I could reach inside the sanctuary and set up the Jews. Some of them were slump-shouldered and actually had sorrowful expressions on their faces, and to this day I have no idea where my mother found a toy store that sold sad, davening action figures. But she did. So the scenario was simple. The Jews want to pray, the Syrians want to kill and pillage, and the Maccabees want to protect the melancholy action figures. It was all about timing. My role was simple and I was very good at it: play God.

Luckily for me, I spent heaps of time in school learning how the almighty, blessed be He, handled things when he lost his temper. You had to first let the drama build. This meant the tiny Jews start their service. All they want to do is pray. Next, you need the Syrians to surround the Temple. After that, you need your Maccabees to get into slaughter formation. And lastly, with the bad guys in the windows and the good guys ready to defend Judea, the war begins. Many die in the battle as God — me — looks down on yet another atrocity in the name of well . . . me. And that's when I step in. One by one I'd start lifting the Syrians by their itty-bitty heads and hurl-

> **My role was simple and I was very good at it: play God.**

ing them across the living room. *AAAAUUUUGGGHHH!* they'd scream as they flew and bounced and rolled under the sofa. My dog, Shana, would chase them and sniff their dead bodies. And in no time, the frightened worshippers inside the Temple would climb to their feet with the help of my mighty hand and once again continue with their prayers. "Thank you, God," they'd say to me as they put their tallises and yarmulkes back on, dusting off their knees. I'd then reach in through the open dome and tap them on their heads with the tip of my thumb. "You're welcome," I'd say in my deepest James Earl Jones voice. "Now cheer up and smile, for Christ's sake. It's Chanukah!"

Creature Comfies

I HAVE A VERY INTERESTING BUSINESS PROPOSITION THAT I THINK WOULD BE PERFECT FOR YOU," MY FATHER TOLD ME OVER THE PHONE. I RECOGNIZED THE TONE IN HIS VOICE FROM TWO YEARS EARLIER, WHEN HE'D SUGGESTED THAT I "START A GAME SHOW" — LIKE *NAME THAT TUNE,* BUT WITH VIDEOS. "FOR THE MTV GENERATION," HE SAID. AS HE IMAGINED IT, I WOULD BE THE PERFECT HOST.

Before we got off the phone, my father told me that a new product had found its way to him from China and that I might be able to help him with it.

A week or so later, we sat down at the Forum Diner in Paramus, New Jersey, to discuss the new product. I had just finished my master's degree in the philosophy of religion at the Harvard Divinity School and was teaching after-school Hebrew school at Central Synagogue in Manhattan. The other teachers were a mix of rabbinical students and singer-songwriters. I took the F train back and forth from Brooklyn, where I lived, rereading my tattered copies of Kierkegaard's *Sickness unto Death* and Rosenzweig's *Star of Redemption*. I was miserable.

My father opened a large shopping bag and pulled out what appeared to be a small, furry teddy bear.

"I call it the Creature Comfy," he said.

I took a closer look. It was a twelve-inch-long band of mohair with small Velcro squares at each end and a stuffed animal fastened to it. Synthetic swatches of white fabric were sewn onto its paws and feet; black plastic eyes and nose were glued to its face.

"I don't get it. It's a scarf attached to a teddy bear?"

"Not a scarf. A muffler." My dad demonstrated by wrapping the Creature Comfy around his own neck. "Scarves are for Eugenes. This makes it cool to keep warm."

Six years of higher education: six years of office hours and highlighters and trying to track down additional readings left on reserve; six years of eight A.M. language labs and sharing a bathroom with the date-raping fraternity on the other side of the hall; six years of teaching fellows who can't read their own writing in the margins of blue books, of attempting to shed my ethnocentric bias, of making quote signs with my fingers, of quote unquote optional review sessions, of selling $45 textbooks back to the college bookstore for $1.50, of girls with Robert Doisneau prints on their walls, of guys who wear Malcolm X hats and whose last names are also the names of campus dorms, of carrying floppy disks to the computer center to print out two-page reaction papers on what Foucault meant by "power."

It had all come to this.

"Are you guys ready to order?" the waitress asked us.

"I'll have the Greek omelet with whole wheat toast."

She turned to my father and waited. And waited. She knew he wasn't dead because his eyes were open and he was sitting in a chair holding a menu.

"The pancakes with fresh banana, blueberries, and raspberries," he read. "How's that served?"

Luckily our waitress was more patient than me.

"The pancakes come with bananas, blueberries, and raspberries on top. It's really good."

"I see." He nodded. "I'll have the pancakes, then."

My father took out a few more Creature Comfies: a monkey that vaguely resembled Curious George, an alligator with a bow tie, and a slanty eyed Santa Claus. "One of my suppliers in China sent these samples to me. I think they have very interesting possibilities. I mean, couldn't you see these becoming a trend?"

"Sure, I mean, I guess," I said. "I mean . . . it seems like a good idea. But what does this have to do with me, Dad?"

"Well, if I'm going to get these into the big department stores, you know, like Nordstrom, Bloomingdale's, and Lord & Taylor, then I'm going to need a salesman. We only have a couple of people working for us and I barely have enough time as it is. . . . I know you want to be a writer, but in the meantime, for money — you need something to support you while you're pursuing your writing, no?"

He had a point. A graduate degree in the philosophy of religion might've opened some doors in ancient Greece, but in New York in 1997, it was an albatross. After a while I had deleted it from my résumé and started telling potential employers that I had spent the past two years bumming around Europe. Other than chasing fourth graders singing songs from *South Park*, I wasn't qualified to do just about anything. In fact, the night before, I'd been bemoaning the fact with my friend Joe Braverman, who lived on the top floor of his parents' brownstone on Seventh Street, around the corner. We were listening to Cypress Hill and he was trying to convince me to apply to dental school with him. Joe had studied philosophy as an undergraduate and was now beginning his second year of a postbac at Columbia.

"Look, just 'cause you've given up on everything you've ever

> A graduate degree in the philosophy of religion might've opened some doors in ancient Greece, but in New York in 1997, it was an albatross.

wanted to do with your life, don't drag me down with you," I protested.

"What are you talking about?" Joe asked as he snorted a line of heroin from the cover of a chemistry textbook, with B-Real boasting, "I ain't goin' out like that" from Joe's childhood cassette player.

"Dreams," I answered. "I'm not ready to give up on all of my dreams at age twenty-five."

"Do you *really* believe the horseshit that comes out of your mouth?" Joe replied. "You don't actually want to be a writer. That just became part of your shtick along the way. To help you get girls or something. What you really want are the things that everybody wants: money, a hot wife, a family. . . . Now pardon me, I have to go vomit."

I wasn't ready to apply to dental school, but Joe's advice was fresh in my mind as I sat before my father at the Forum Diner. I needed to start thinking about my future. Up to that point, I had prided myself on not making sacrifices, not giving a second thought to what was practical. During "shopping week" of every semester of college, I would visit classes like Basic Finance or Intro to Programming, only to opt out at the last second for yet another seminar on Lacan or the Seminole Indians. Over a hundred thousand dollars had gone into my education. What skills did I have to show for it?

"Would I have to come into the office?" I asked my father.

"Not necessarily. Basically, you would be in charge of making relationships with the buyers at the big department stores. You're good at making relationships. You have so many friends. It's not an easy thing. I could never have as many friends as you do. It's a skill you have, really."

"I'm sure it's a lot harder than just making friends. I mean, these are big corporations."

"Look, when my parents got to the United States in 1940, before they started the zipper business, they used to sell sweaters. Papa was in sportswear in Vienna, and when they got to New York he and his brother bought an old machine that would knit sweaters. Then he brought the sweaters to Macy's. I'm sure you're right. I'm sure it's not that simple, but if it was that simple, I wouldn't need you."

Our food arrived. My father frowned.

"What's this?" my father asked the waitress.

"You ordered the pancakes."

"But there's only one pancake here. I ordered pan*cakes*."

"Do you want something else, sir?"

"No, that's all right. I'll make do."

OVER THE NEXT two weeks I tried to turn myself into a salesman. It felt like that ridiculous Eddie Murphy skit where he turns himself into a white guy and applies for a loan and the guy at the bank just hands him bags and bags of cash for free.

I mean, how the hell was I going to fool anybody into thinking that I was a salesman?

I took out my earrings and had some business cards printed up at Kinko's. I tried on the suit I got for my first college interview, eight years earlier.

I called Bloomingdale's, Lord & Taylor, Macy's, and Nordstrom to find out who did the buying for their children's apparel and accessories departments. I collected names and numbers. I left messages with assistants. I said I was "Joshua Neuman of Royal Slides, Sales Co." and that I was calling "Re: the Creature Comfy." I left my number in Brooklyn and warned my roommate, Ari, that I might be getting some business calls.

> **Believe it or not, the demand for critics of Hegel's phenomenology has subsided in the last hundred years.**
>
> ∽✎∾

I left message after message. The calls never came. "Are you sure you gave her the message? . . . I have a very exciting product that would be a perfect gift for Christmas or Chanukah." I imagined Kierkegaard and Rosenzweig frowning at my crass commodification of Christianity and Judaism.

Screw Kierkegaard and Rosenzweig. How would they support themselves as writers today? Believe it or not, the demand for critics of Hegel's phenomenology has subsided in the last hundred years. If Kierkegaard were alive today he'd be hocking Legos in Copenhagen. Rosenzweig would be in med school.

I called my father. It was already October. Neither of us seemed to have any idea that the buying for the coming holiday season would have been done by the prior January.

"You need to meet with them face-to-face. Make a visual impression."

"Do I just show up at their office?"

"Listen, there is no simple answer," he replied. "I wish I could tell you the ABC's, but they don't exist. This opportunity isn't going to be there forever. I remember the time I was about to seal that nylon-zipper deal with Pillowtex and YKK beat me to the punch."

I thought of my grandfather as a refugee in 1940, with a wife, three children, little money, barely speaking English, heading to Macy's with his sweaters. I thought of the fresh memories of the war that must have been in his mind. I couldn't just give up. If the buyers weren't going to come to me, I was going to have to go to them.

I started with Macy's, which was, I learned, along with Bloomingdale's, part of a larger company called "Federated." I carried the Creature Comfies in an old suitcase I had used throughout my childhood when my family went on summer vacations. I took the F train to Thirty-fourth Street and then the elevator to the fourth floor, where the Children's Apparel Division was headquartered.

"I'm here to see Katherine Akers," I informed the receptionist. The name was easy to remember because it was so close to Kathy Acker, the sex-positive feminist writer.

"Do you have an appointment?"

What would my grandfather have done?

I pried open my suitcase, reached in, and handed an Asiatic Curious George to the receptionist.

"This is the Creature Comfy."

She undid the Velcro and somewhat miraculously knew to wrap it around her neck.

"It's a scarf?"

"It's a muffler. . . . I was hoping for just five minutes with Ms. Acker."

Fuck, I said "Acker."

"Ms. Akers is in a meeting, but if you want to leave a sample, I can give it to her along with your contact information."

"Wow, that'd be great." I handed her my business card.

I NEVER DID HEAR back from the buyer of children's apparel and accessories at Macy's. I left two messages, once with Ari letting out a loud burp in the background. Neither Bloomingdale's nor Bergdorf returned any of my messages. Short of standing on Canal Street alongside pirated videotapes and fake Fendi bags, all I could do was try to contact Beverly Shore at Lord & Taylor.

Unlike Macy's, Bloomingdale's, and Bergdorf, the corporate

headquarters of Lord & Taylor is in the same building as its store. So I went to scout out the children's apparel and accessories before making my unsolicited sales pitch to Beverly Shore. While rummaging through some Powerpuff Girls backpacks I noticed two swinging doors below an EMPLOYEES ONLY sign. Wait, I thought, this could be too good to be true: Suppose those doors led to the innermost sanctum? Suppose they led straight to Beverly Shore?

I realize now that spotting the EMPLOYEES ONLY sign at Lord & Taylor was a turning point in my efforts to transform myself into a salesman. Sure, I had tried to pass myself off as someone I was not, but never had I trespassed or broken any other law in the process. Nevertheless, the thought of *not* sneaking through the swinging doors below the EMPLOYEES ONLY sign did not occur to me.

I imagined clinking glasses of champagne with my father and late grandfather, my grandfather making a toast, in his German accent, to our new Creature Comfy empire, my father complaining that his glass wasn't clean. I imagined myself, twenty-five years older, presiding over that empire: the Creature Comfy Saturday morning cartoon, the Creature Comfy breakfast cereal, the Creature Comfy skyscraper in Times Square with a retractable Velcro roof—and it all would begin at this one moment in the children's apparel and accessories department of Lord & Taylor in Manhattan in November 1997.

To be honest, the next couple of minutes are kind of a blur: I walk through the swinging doors. I notice that everyone on this side of the doors has identification badges. I find a staircase. I find an employee directory. I find Beverly Shore's name. I find another set of elevators. I assume that "419" means she is on the fourth floor. I press "4." I get out of the elevator.

I didn't expect that when the doors of the elevator opened I would actually be *inside* Beverly Shore's office. But I was. Sort of.

I was inside lots of offices — at least fifty or sixty cubicles crowded together in a labyrinth-like configuration, probably a hundred Lord & Taylor employees, plus me in the suit from my college interview with the suitcase and a dozen stuffed animals, each attached to a twelve-inch band of mohair.

Each cubicle had a number: 408, 409, 410 . . . I was actually going to come face-to-face with the buyer of children's apparel and accessories . . . 411, 412, 413 . . . millions of children throughout this country would for the first time enjoy keeping their throats and necks covered during the coldest months of the winter . . . 414, 415, 416 . . . in your face, Katherine Akers . . . 417, 418, 419!

Beverly Shore's empty cubicle caught me by surprise. What now? Do I wait? Do I leave a Creature Comfy in front of her monitor with my business card propped in its paws? Do I look for someone else from children's apparel and accessories?

"Can I help you?"

I turned around. A young woman in a business suit, holding a Styrofoam cup.

"Yes, I'm looking for Beverly Shore."

"I'm Beverly Shore," she replied with not a little bit of hesitation.

"My name is Joshua Neuman."

I fumbled with my suitcase, got down on one knee and opened it up, and two or three of the Creature Comfies tumbled out. I picked them up and held up a Mickey Mouse rip-off—an intellectual property litigator's wet dream.

She looked at me as if I was a retarded man showing her my collection of string. I had planned to say, "I would like to introduce you to the Creature Comfy," but the only thing that came out was "Uh, Creature Comfy."

"You don't belong here. I'm going to call security."

The funny thing was that while we were waiting for security to arrive, I had ample opportunity to rebound, to put her at ease, to make my pitch. That's what a real salesman would have done. But as much as I wanted to make my father proud, find a direction in life and get the Creature Comfy on the shelves of department stores across America, all I could feel during those moments was *bad for her*. I imagined what it must have felt like for her to experience this awkward twenty-five-year-old with his suitcase materializing in her place of work, brandishing bizarro versions of Mickey, Minnie, and Curious George. So instead of showing her how the Velcro held both ends together and trying one on, I just stood there with my eyes lowered, waiting for security to escort me out of the building.

Christmas and Chanukah overlapped that year, so when I went home for the holiday, virtually every house on our block but ours was glowing with green and red Christmas lights — thousand-watt suburban altars of excess. The kids on the block were out having a snowball fight, laughing and screaming, all of their necks exposed. I remembered when I was one of them and I used to spot my father turning the corner I was now turning, briefcase in hand, exhausted from doing zipper business — the loving smile I could see envelop his face the moment he spotted me.

My father and I had missed the holiday rush, though no competitor, to the best of my knowledge, has since snatched up the Creature Comfies and turned them into an empire. I entered my parents' house, took off my shoes, and dumped the Creature Comfies on the floor of the living room. Who was I kidding? I wasn't a salesman — if I was really going to be a writer I wasn't going to be a successful salesman on the side. I wasn't going to be a successful anything *on the side.*

> **Who was I kidding? I wasn't a salesman—if I was really going to be a writer I wasn't going to be a successful salesman on the side.**
>
> ❧

That night, my father, mother, brother, and I lit the menorah —
the menorah my grandfather had bought for my parents in Israel in the early 1970s. We kept it in the window "for all the
world to see," though it was hard to imagine the light from these
two flimsy candles from ShopRite being noticed by anyone on a
street glowing like the Vegas Strip.

I stared into the fire and thought about the suitcase, Søren
Kierkegaard and Franz Rosenzweig, the suit from my college
interview, the potential infringements upon international copy-
right law, the look on the face of Beverly Shore as I stood in her
cubicle, and whether the holes where my hoop earrings used
to hang had closed up for good. I thought about my late grandfather, my father, and I standing in front of that same menorah,
singing the same prayers every year and dreaming of empires as
our neighbors burned watts and drank eggnog, never giving a
second thought to the neck warmth of America's children.

Week at a Glance

I.

I'S SIMULTANEOUSLY THE FIRST NIGHT OF CHANUKAH, MY PAPA IRWIN'S NINETY-EIGHTH BIRTHDAY, AND CHRISTMAS, THE LAST WEEK OF 2005. I AM HOME IN L.A. FOR A VISIT, MY FIRST IN A GOOD LONG WHILE. IT'S A CELEBRATORY CLUSTER-FUCK, AND MY MOTHER IS HOSTING A PARTY.

"We light one candle tonight, for the first night, and this other candle is called the *shamash*," she explains in a voice usually reserved for kindergarteners.

Present are my father and stepmother, my brother and his wife, some cousins, my mother, Papa, and me. Things are a wee bit tense, for many boring and complicated family-issue reasons, all of which boil down to *I don't want to be here.*

My brother's wife is invited to light the menorah, which is pretty straightforward since it's only the first night and there is therefore only the one single candle to light. My brother is wearing a pair of two-hundred-dollar jeans that first appeared around the time he and his beloved miraculously found each other on JDate. I'm feeling fairly homicidal, but I sing thinly along with the *bracha*.

By the soup course, the man of the hour — Papa Irwin, not Jesus — is nodding off at the foot of the table, a depressing paper party hat resting asymmetrically on his head. One cousin is totally trashed and keeps telling me that I have sadness inside me and that she therefore would like to hypnotize me. A teenaged cousin smiles shyly and repeats, "What up, Carrie Bradshaw?" ostensibly because I live in New York and spend a good deal of my time having cocktails with the girls, sleeping with strangers, and lounging around my apartment staring at my laptop. Throughout dinner my brother's wife unwraps and feeds him pieces of chocolate gelt. She eats no gelt, not because she doesn't love money — quite the contrary! — but because she is anorexic.

> **If I could nap through family time I'd probably enjoy being around my family a great deal.**

I feel empty and morose, and strangely enough not even my gift-wrapped copy of this year's *Best American Short Stories*

(Thanks, Mom!) makes things better. I wonder whether I should wake up Papa so that he can enjoy his party, but he's probably happier asleep, and I'm more than a little jealous. If I could nap through family time I'd probably enjoy being around my family a great deal.

I excuse myself before birthday cake is served and lie on a dew-covered chaise in the dark backyard. It seems I have a voice message, the blinking red light on my cell like a beacon of hope. It's from an inebriated friend, himself home for a visit in the Midwest, wishing me a "Shabbat shalom, motherfucker!" which is funny, since, of course, it's not Shabbat. "I'm calling all the Jews in my phone," he says. "But you're the only Jew in my phone, so really I'm only calling you!" This is sufficiently uplifting, and I spend the rest of the evening trying to relax on the chaise, fruitlessly searching for even one star in the Los Angeles night sky.

A Happy Chanukah to one and all.

II.

After last night's circus of despair, I forgo the candles ritual tonight. I have no plans and I'm in too crappy a mood for polite company. Oh, and it's the day after Christmas! So the Western world feels shut down, desolate, totally depressing. There is only one thing to be done.

Every Jew and his mother are seeing *Munich* tonight. What this means, I realize belatedly, is that I am trapped in the sold-out theater alongside roughly half of heeb L.A. How did I not foresee this? Inevitably, I run into several dozen friends of my parents'. And my ex-father-in-law, who proffers a small wave and thereafter avoids eye contact. (Which, interestingly enough, is not so very unlike how it felt being married to his son.)

"Are you here by yourself?" asks the fourth or fifth family acquaintance I run into. I feel completely pitiful. Christmas is a time for Jews to see movies *together*.

"No," I lie. Then I duck back into the crowd, muttering something about finding my friends.

I locate a single seat next to a benign older couple who, thankfully, don't look the least bit familiar. They endear themselves to me twenty minutes into the film by nonchalantly passing me the popcorn. I have found my friends after all. When the lights come up at the end, the husband is white-knuckled with rage. "What'd you think?" I ask him. As Maestro Spielberg himself has pointed out, this movie is something of a Rorschach test for divergent Semitic passions. The man doesn't disappoint.

"I'll tell you something," he says, fury cutting away at every word. "It ain't a picnic being a Jew after Auschwitz." I want to point out that it probably wasn't a picnic to be a Jew *during* Auschwitz either, but I just nod emphatically as he goes on about counterterrorism not being morally equivalent to terrorism. I (violently) disagree, but I cannot afford to alienate my new friends, not when there's a minefield of family acquaintances still filing out of the theater. He and his wife promise to buy my forthcoming book; I wish them a Happy Chanukah. And voilà! The left and the right have called a special holiday truce.

III.

My mother's Havurah has its annual Chanukah party. The Havurah is a group of friends who meet once a month to schmooze, eat, and talk about books and politics. Even though I live three thousand miles away and don't have all that much to say to anyone, I've known these people and their children for about as long as I can remember, and I'm increasingly grateful for this kind of continuity.

It's a bustling party, a warm, lively, colorful gathering with food-laden tables and adorable children underfoot and a gigantic pile of gifts by the fireplace. Its resemblance to anything I've experienced of late in my own family home is minimal. When we arrive, the three candles in several *Chanukiot* are already burning in the window, casting a further glow on the proceedings.

The traditional gift exchange (also known as a Yankee Swap, but insert joke about tightfisted Jews here) goes something like this: Everyone brings a gift costing fifteen dollars or so. We draw numbers out of a hat. Number one picks a gift and opens it. Number two can either swipe number one's gift or choose another gift to open. And so on down the line. It's best, in this game, to pick a high number out of the hat, so that you can see everything that's already been opened and take your pick. Fortunes can be won or lost in an instant. I am excited to draw a whopping 17.

There's a scented candle assortment, a neat baking kit with novelty cookie cutters, an M. C. Escher book, a T-shirt reading KISH MIR IN TUCHES!, and then someone opens the gift I know I will claim as my own: an oh-so-apropos humor book called *50 Relatives Worse Than Yours.*

Later, on the way to the bathroom, I duck into a carpeted hallway lined with photos: wedding photos, portraits of the grandparents as young men and women, baby photos, the whole nine. Like all family photos (others' and my own), they fill me with unwieldy bitterness and hard-core longing all at once. My favorite of the little kids, a porky eighteen-month-old with a six-hundred-word vocabulary, comes toddling down the hall in a rainbow onesie, holding fast to a jelly doughnut. The last time I saw this child she was in utero, and the next time I see her she'll probably be a bat mitzvah, but no matter. "Hi!" she says. I grab and kiss-attack her and pretend to munch on her belly. She cracks up and we return to the party together. There are things I covet that, alas, can't be grasped with even the highest Yankee Swap number.

My friend Heather, also in town visiting her own family, picks me up. We go for Mexican food in her mother's car and listen to ancient CDs of a local Jewish pop star whose relentlessly earnest, heavily synthesized musicalizations of various prayers and parables have earned him a die-hard fan base of Jewish housewives all over Southern California. Heather and I share a secret past of having been members of this man's preteen chorus army, when we were each sort of voluntarily molested by, respectively, a much older teen and another aspiring Jewish pop singer. We sing along, doing the cheese-ball jazz-hand choreography as we remember it, more or less exactly like when we where thirteen.

IV.

Today I fly to Seattle to spend the rest of the week with two of my best friends: Sarah and Jackie. Jackie and I both live in New York, but Sarah's in medical school out here, so we three haven't gotten to spend any quality time together in a while.

After some requisite gaping at the Space Needle, the lush, hilly views, and the stunning multitude of lovely coffee shops and cafés around town, Sarah takes us to a Chanukah party hosted by friends of hers, an engaged couple.

The guy is Jewish, but the kind of Jewish that seems to back away from itself: not *Jewish*, mind you, just Jew-*ish*. A real fan-of-Seinfeld kind of Jew (*not that there's anything wrong with that*). His fiancée is not a Jew but has spent the last three days making latkes. She explains how at first they were too soggy because she'd used too much egg. Then she scrapped that batch and started from scratch. But the frying itself was tricky, so half of the second batch had to be tossed. She wanted the latkes to be perfect. She really respects Jewish culture, and it was important to her that the latkes come out right. The latkes, needless to say, seem pretty loaded (and I don't mean with applesauce and sour cream, either).

"Are you guys Jewish?" she asks us politely.

"Hell, no," we say, shaking our heads in jest at the distasteful-ness of such a thought. (Then, when it's clear that irony has no place here, we feel bad. "Yes. We're Jewish," Jackie says. "And the latkes look great!" "Do they?" our hostess asks anxiously. "Latkes are hard for everyone," I reassure her.)

When it comes time to light the menorah, our hosts cast about helplessly. It becomes quickly apparent that Jackie and Sarah and I, along with the affianced guy, are the only children of Israel at this Chanukah party. "Don't look at me," Sarah says, backing away from the menorah like a vampire from a cross. Jackie and I — Jewish day school refugees, both — have a brief argument over whether tonight's four candles go on the right or the left. I think they go on the right; she thinks the left.

"Rabbi Hillel said the right and Rabbi Shammai said the left, so it's fine either way," Jackie says, with more than a trace of sarcasm.

"Wow," someone says. "You guys really *are* Jewish."

We sing the *bracha* alone and embarrassedly, like we're on display at the mall next to a giant tree, a cardboard menorah, and a fat old biker dressed up as Santa. People! Chanukah is really not that big a deal, religiously speaking. If it didn't happen to fall around the same time as the good old alleged virgin birth, Ross from *Friends* probably wouldn't even know about it! Will our hosts be throwing a Sukkot dinner in their back-yard? A Tisha b'Av study session? A Purim hoedown? I think not. So why, in the absence of any other Jewish observance or iden-tity, this big, blue-and-white-streamered, latke-obsessed Chanukah thing?

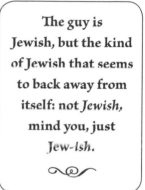

The guy is Jewish, but the kind of Jewish that seems to back away from itself: not *Jewish*, mind you, just *Jew-ish*.

V.

By some Maccabee miracle, Jackie and I have scored a pair of below-market tickets on Craigslist to tonight's sold-out Sleater-Kinney show at the Showbox. What a day we're having: stroll-ing, shopping, eating, laughing. I love this city, it's official. And I love my friends! And now we're seeing my favorite band at a storied Seattle concert venue! For eighteen bucks! Which is also *chai*! Life does not get much better. But for the fact that my si-nuses still hurt a little bit after having expelled lemonade from my nostrils at dinner when Jackie made me laugh too hard recounting a comedy routine she saw recently (in which David Cross poked fun at misuse of the word *literally,* as in "I *literally* shit my pants!" or "My brother's wife *literally* has an ass for a face!" or "My boss is *literally* retarded!"), I am having a grand time.

We are busy dancing and sipping vodka tonics when the amazing Carrie Brownstein, between spectacular sets, makes mention of the big C:

"So tonight's Chanukah," she says to the crowd, fiddling with the knobs on her guitar. There are few cheers. It's a wonderful thing to belong quite so completely to my surroundings. This is what life is for, I think: to be a living, breathing, contradictory mess *and* belong entirely.

Janet Weiss, the drummer, concurs. "Yeah."

"I think it's like the fifth night," Brownstein says.

"Woooo-hooooo!" yells a guy nearby.

"Sixth!" I shout, just to participate, but then realize that I am wrong. It matters not.

"Sixth? Fifth?" Carrie asks. "Shit, I don't know. I can't be trusted with these things." And with that the ladies rip into "Rollercoaster" (or maybe it was "Dig Me Out," I can't remember; I can't be trusted with these things).

We forget to light candles tonight, as it's two A.M. by the time the show's over and of course it's raining and we're pretty buzzed, so as soon as we manage to find a cab back to Sarah's, we hightail it woozily to bed.

VI.

We get into a fight today. Sarah feels left out because Jackie and I share a life in New York; I feel left out because Sarah and Jackie wake up hours earlier than I do and go running together (why would anyone *do* such a thing?); Jackie's annoyed because Sarah's annoyed; Sarah's annoyed because Jackie's annoyed; I'm annoyed because Sarah only grudgingly indulges my vegetarianism; and so on. It's not so much a fight as a crossing of wires, a tripping of multiple overlapping insecurities and anxieties. Finally things boil over and we have a good cry, profess our collective undying love and affection, and immediately feel better. Typical girl bullshit. The truth of it is, my friends are my family (see also: Night I).

I consider Sarah my cosmic reward for having made it through a decade at Jewish summer camp. We shared a bunk bed when we were eleven, and we got into a fistfight that year. (I won, Sarah; you know I did.) Our time at this Jewish summer camp was the source of much angst for me (and, later, much grist for the writing mill). It was a pretty soulless place. We often reminisce ruefully about the time we, along with all the other adolescent girls at camp, were formally lectured by a kindly and quite well-respected rabbi about the importance of marrying as early as possible and starting a family, and about how prioritizing career and/or self-actualization would mean not only that we would die barren and alone but that the Jewish people, also, would cease to exist.

Tonight Sarah is hosting Shabbat dinner, so we go to the market and shop for supplies. My contribution will be my signature vegan cupcakes, which are not remotely as unappetizing as they may sound, I swear to God (there is banana involved). In the frosting aisle, I pick up sugar letters (the whole alphabet, in triplicate!) and rainbow jimmies for cupcake adornment.

The Shabbat crowd is made up of Sarah's housemates and several of their friends, most of whom are weekly regulars. I can't overstate the wonder and joy of finding like-minded people gathered here for Shabbat, for Chanukah, for eating and hanging out. It's that most rare of religious phenomena: organic. One of Sarah's friends rolls two enormous blunts ("For après-Shabbos," he says with a grin). In the kitchen, her housemates are ritually washing their hands while they make up an intricate rap — two play human beat box while the third interweaves the *bracha* and something about his "Shabbos bitches" — about, yes, ritual hand washing. Jackie watches them, agape.

"They're always doing that," Sarah sighs.

First we light the menorah, and tonight everyone in the room knows the words and sings loudly along. Then we light the Shabbat candles, with, again, everyone join-ing in. Then we feast. Then we smoke the blunts. "In the basement!" Sarah in-sists. "But it's Shabbos!" we plead. She relents.

When I go into the kitchen to frost the cupcakes I find Jackie already ar-ranging the pink sugar letters into words on each one. She's diligently arranged "fun hole," "eat me," "tits," "poop," "ass wipe," "fuck," "balls," "jizz," and a couple others even I won't repeat. Sounds infantile, maybe, but in our col

> **Is this what our parents had in mind for us when they chauffeured us to Hebrew school and bat mitzvah lessons? Pornographic vegan cupcakes, Shabbos blunts? I must say that I think so.**
>
> ෨෧

lective state of gladness they are the height of wit and creativity. Especially, of course, as the letter supply dwindles and we are forced to be extra inventive with spelling.

Is this what our parents had in mind for us when they chauf-feured us to day school, Hebrew school, and bat mitzvah les-sons? Is this what they hoped for when they waved good-bye and sent us off to that Lord of the Yid Flies summer camp? Por-nographic vegan cupcakes, Shabbos blunts, *al netilat yadayim* woven intricately into a rap in a house high up on a hill in the Pacific Northwest? I must say that I think so. At first glance, the above might seem like religious perversion, but scratch the surface and you'll see a roomful of young Jews claiming that identity in the context of countless other identities. Dig deeper and you'll find a roomful of Jews owning Judaism — and loving it — in a way no easy parochial regurgitation or rote spawning could ever approach. Oh, how I wish that kindly and completely misguided old rabbi could be here with us now. If we could bottle this and sell it, surely we'd be knee-deep in Jewish continuity-hysteria-foundation grants. And just imagine the weed that would buy!

VII.

Another party tonight: New Year's Eve, though it's difficult to get all that amped up about a milestone so traditionally over-loaded with good-time pressure. Every year it's the same, the anticlimax so much more prevalent than the purported climax. (Like hooking up with a future Jewish pop star. Or whatever.)

Sarah's friends from medical school arrive in clusters. A future anesthesiologist has brought the board game Cranium, which we are to play as the evening's entertainment. A future neurosurgeon bears a bottle of champagne in each fist. A future gynecologist brings her gangly, fifteen-year-old brother, because he had no other plans and she couldn't bear to leave him home alone for the last/first few hours of 2005/06.

Two old friends of Jackie's join the party too, thankfully rounding out the left-brain contingent. We four form a Cranium team, as the med students want no part of our liberal arts asses.

The med students also Just Say No, which means that our team at first appears to be at something of a disadvantage.

Here's a piece of advice: don't ever play Cranium with a bunch of medical students. Especially don't ever play Cranium with medical students if you are a) someone with an iota of perspective on board games, b) someone with an iota of perspective on competition in general, c) extremely stoned, or d) all of the above.

We are incapable of taking the game seriously, which frustrates our furrowed-browed, adorably Type A opponents to no end. While they huddle together and strategize, we gleefully sing rounds of "Light one candle for the Maccabee soldiers, with thanks that their light didn't die! Light one candle for the pain they endured when their right to exist was denied!" We lose track of whose turn it is. We shout out answers to other teams' questions, trying to be helpful and sportsmanlike. And, eventually, we legitimately win the game. This is infuriating to the losers, whose losing is almost enough to incite the kind of existential crisis usually sparked by fatal botched diagnoses in residency. They've lost Cranium to a bunch of *stoners*?!

"Good game. Congratulations," they say tightly.

By then it's about eleven fifty-five, so we head out to the street with noisemakers and pots and pans, looking out over the city and the Space Needle, where fireworks will signify the end of the year.

Unbeknownst to us, the fifteen-year-old has been drinking champagne all night, and he starts vomiting his brains out (not literally) pretty soon after we welcome the New Year.

Once again we've forgotten the candles.

VIII.

We almost forget all about the eighth and final night, too.

When we finally do remember, just before bed, we load up the whole menorah together, no debate tonight about where the candles go. We set it in the window, the rest of the house dark and quiet. It is the first day of 2006 and tomorrow we'll all go back to our lives: Sarah to three months of internal medicine rotation in the middle of Idaho, Jackie and I to Chelsea and Brooklyn, respectively. It's going to be a big year for each of us: lots of changes and miracles and stepping-stones and new challenges we vaguely know are on their way. And who knows when we'll all be together again?

I am nominated to hold the *shamash*, which I find I'm excited to do, like when I was little and it felt like a great honor. I light the candles from left to right, starting with the newest and lighting one for each of the past seven nights as I go.

First is tonight's, eight, with my girls beside me and the sound of Seattle rain gently pelting the window under our three tone-deaf, exhausted voices. Then last night's, seven, and the collective ruckus we made banging our pots and pans to usher in a new year while fireworks exploded over the city. Six, Shabbos blunts and porno-cakes. Five at Sleater-Kinney. Four as token, pseudomissionary Jews in a roomful of well-intentioned holiday whores. Three at the Havurah party. Two alone at the movies. And by the time I make it to the last candle, the first night, Christmas, my uniquely fraught family and my uniquely fraught place in (or out of) it, I'm almost able to own even that. It's been a good week, it's a new year now, after all, and the whole menorah is glowing, full, finally complete.

Jackie and Sarah and I stand looking for a moment at the blazing menorah and its reflection in the window. Above it our faces are reflected, too. We linger for a moment and then we turn away, off into a new week, a new year, and a blessedly blank slate.

Chanukah Your Hearts Out!

*A sermonette on the proper role of the holiday
in the lives of modern atheist Jews*

... I SPEAK NOW TO THOSE OF YOU WHO GREW UP
IN THE HAZE OF MODERN SECULAR LIFE, WHO, LIKE
ME, DERIVE FROM THE SHTETLS OF THE PALE STEPPES,
FROM LUBLIN AND MINSK, FROM BEARDED MEN WHO
SPENT HOURS IN COLD STONE HALLS HUNCHED OVER
LAW, WHO FOUND IN GOD AND HIS IRASCIBLE TINKER-
ING THE SUBJECT OF AN ENTIRE LIFE, AND NEVER ONCE
QUESTIONED THE WORD.

I speak to you, the children and grandchildren and great-
grandchildren of these men, who have known no other life but

suburban America with its bright avenues and TV shows and bubble gum, with its idle afternoons, its pieties of plenitude. I speak to those of you who, like me, have fallen away from God, or never knew Him, the ones who snored through Sunday school, who learned bits of blessings at sex-starved summer camps, who became strangers to the shul, and learned to regard the Almighty as a lunatic superstition.

I speak to those of you who consider the essential miracle to be consciousness, our ability to perceive ourselves, to demystify the world we inhabit, to pursue our fraught paths toward happiness.

I speak to each of you today, my brethren and sistren — my scattered flock! my wayward tribe! — and I say the following:

Look not with derision upon the festival of Chanukah.

Neither mock the holiday with jokes or silly songs, nor dismiss it as a triviality trumped up to match the retail onslaught of Christmas. Let not these days pass as any others might, as if you were like any other person. You are not. We are not.

For all our wanderings, all our silent disavowals, all our half-acknowledged shame, we are Jews. The sons and daughters of Abraham. Abraham, whose grand delusion was of a singular benevolent father. Abraham, whose folly resided in the belief that one bloodline might hold the franchise on divine approval. Abraham, who nearly smote his own boy out of dumb loyalty.

And yet remember: we need not endorse the savagery of our

holy book to recognize the beauty in its ideas. Consider the story of the Maccabees, insurgent rebels who came to believe that God carried them into battle, who fell under the spell of sanctified violence and turned their enemies into lakes of blood and reclaimed the Temple, then were slaughtered too. Madmen, of course, but ones illumi-

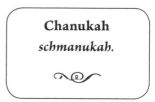

Chanukah
schmanukah.

nated from within by personal sacrifice, spiritual devotion, and valor.

This *is* our legacy, comrades. There is no separating the noble from the wicked within us. We are trapped by circumstances of history, often forced to make bad choices. We need look no further than our own promised land, in this very age, for proof.

It would surely be easier for us, as modern Jews — fully assimilated! credit-approved! — to disavow the tangled skein of our history. Chanukah *schmanukah*, we might say. More propaganda from the home office. Let the holiday slip past, like so much wind-blown tinsel. But, you see, we are not tinsel. We are a family, the children of monotheism. To ignore this essential fact of our being would be to unmoor us from our own legacy and cast us adrift in time.

It is true what the pop psychologists say: we don't get to choose our family. Our only choice resides in how we treat them. Do we assume a posture of convenience and self-regard? Or of gratitude and humility? To put this another way: Do we choose to acknowledge who and where we come from? Do we honor those whose sacrifices vouchsafed our own outrageous freedoms?

Today I exhort you, my fellow fallow Jews, to treat Chanukah this year with more dignity than perhaps it deserves. On each of the eight nights, prepare a meal and gather your loved ones to you. Turn off all electronic devices. Allow yourself the high cholesterol latke, the sour cream and applesauce. You need not light candles or sing the prayer, but you must dispense a blessing, one at least, each night.

> That's what being Jewish is: summoning the means to question who you are and how you have behaved.
>
> ～❧～

Above all, you must reflect on those whose love binds you to this world, if you have done right by them, if you have been good to those in need of goodness, and spoken against those who would do this goodness harm.

That's what being Jewish is: summoning the means to question who you are and how you have behaved. Have you remained alight in the darkness of cruel wishes, like a lamp in an ancient temple? Have you forgiven? Have you lived up to the standards of your one and only heart?

It is still possible, after all, to forge a covenant that binds us not to God in obedience but to one another in mercy. We need only choose, this year, to keep the flame lit . . .

The Guinea Pig

ANIC, PURE AND UNADULTERATED, WAS WHAT MADE ME WANT A NEW DOG. I THOUGHT SURELY A DOG WOULD PROTECT ME, BUT EVERY PLEA WAS MET WITH THE SAME RESPONSE.

"That's a whole lot of responsibility," my mother said.

"For me," my father said.

"For me you mean," my mother said.

Until one November day when I was eight years old, my mother suggested another kind of animal.

"One that doesn't shed or need to be walked," she said. "How does that sound?"

"Sounds like the perfect Christmas gift," my father said.

"Please," my mother said. "Stop it."

This was no different than any other holiday season in our home.

Perhaps here is where I should mention that my 100 percent Jewish father was — and remains — obsessed with Christmas. He decorated the mantle with his Christmas cards, hung candy canes from boughs of evergreens, taped mistletoe at every threshold, mulled his wine, and tried to get my mother to submit to an evergreen — and very tasteful, adorned with only one red velvet ribbon — wreath on the door.

"No!" she'd say. "I can't live with that, I just can't."

My mother grew up in a Jewish household. My grandfather, a judge, had studied to be a rabbi. And Nana was on the committee of the new Reform temple in her town.

> **Perhaps here is where I should mention that my 100 percent Jewish father was—and remains—obsessed with Christmas.**
>
> ∾℘〜

"Well, it's very important to me," he'd tell her, tilting his head and hanging the wreath anyway. Though both of my father's parents were Jewish — from Western Europe, they proudly proclaimed — he and his sisters had not been raised observant. Recently, however, his father had turned quite religious, joining a Conservative synagogue in San Diego, where he and my grandmother had recently moved for their retirement. My father couldn't stand to hear him talk of it, of God, or of the way he kept kosher — but for the raw oysters my father would offer up to him, his father's approval given in the way he gobbled them up, then turned around sheepishly to see if any of us were looking.

"I don't understand how Christmas could be so important to you," my mother said.

"It's part of my history," my father replied. "I grew up in Minneapolis and I remember the lights on the streets, the lighted trees, the wreaths. It was always magical."

My mother crossed her arms. "Have your holiday stuff inside," she said. "But no wreath. Nothing outside this house." Ludicrous, she'd call him as he searched the many cabinets in my room for the photos that were evidence he had celebrated Christmas when he was young. "We're Jews, for Chrissake," my mother would say.

I WAS A GIRL with many secrets. By day I was a normal child in suburban Washington, D.C., and as day turned to twilight, my panic began until, by evening and then night, it had morphed into near panic. The spark that caught the flame of my fear was my sister's birth, when I was five. Her arrival propelled me out of my room next door to my parents' and up to the attic to make space for her. Moving to the attic seemed like a great idea at first, not least of all because the room had a window seat that looked out onto our suburban D.C. street, and a wall of cabinets that housed strange and unusual objects beneath its many doors: my father's old oil paints and horsehair brushes, tiny canvases thick with cracking paint, my mother's girlhood diaries, a list of boys — Jeffrey Seltzer, Martin Finkelstein, Harry Lefkowitz — written in careful script on the back of each one. Every cabinet of that wall was a window to who my parents once were, or perhaps more to what they had wanted — intended? — to become. And in the storage space beneath the window there were my mother's antique dolls.

A child of the seventies — or, rather, a child with an ERA-abiding working mother in the seventies — I was not allowed to have dolls or any gender-specific toys. Pulling these strange dolls out from beneath the removable, nearly hidden seat, with their broken porcelain faces, foreheads stuck with hair, exposed scalps, and yellowing satin dresses and frayed cotton shirts, was nothing short of thrilling.

But in the end the dolls could not protect me from my lonely new life in the attic. Those dolls lay in wait, and I imagined their burgeoning rage at being left beneath the window seat. There were other things: a woman in flames screaming from a burning house that I had inadvertently watched on television with a babysitter, as well as the swamp thing she had watched one afternoon. And there was my sister's constant screaming, over which was juxtaposed my parent's arguing, a noise that worsened as the decade moved along.

And in those moments I yearned for a puppy, another heart-

beat in my room, something to give me comfort while protect-
ing me from the dolls, who had all lost their once-good looks,
and whose anger at being wrapped in old paper and stuffed in a
secret compartment was sure to break them out of there. Would
they come for me? A dog would surely anticipate such an attack
and protect me in a way, it became increasingly clear, my parents never could.

WOULD THIS HOLIDAY bring me a creature with whom
to share my life? Christmas seemed to me just another reason
for my parents to fight: you do more, no I do more, you work late,
no I work late, you love Christmas, no I do. But now I see it as
the singular cause of these fights: a different way of looking out
at the world and a different idea of how the world looks back.

These arguments grew into full-fledged fights over the way
my father's family tried to cover up being Jewish. They were
German Jews, not the Eastern European stock from which my
mother hailed, and my mother believed they thought themselves above being Jewish. She told me that at their wedding,
my father's grandmother (who had by then become a Christian
Scientist!) had told my father, Better you had married a shiksa
than a Polish Jew.

But what child growing up in this country does not appreciate Christmas? It is what we see on television, in the movies, in
theaters and schools and the novels we read. Who doesn't want

to be a part of this? We went to temple on Rosh Hashanah and Yom Kippur, but we also hid Easter eggs. The story to me *then* was in the latter: what did you *get*? Was my father trying to give me every experience, or was he, too, ruled by a kind of fear, fear about what not having a standard American childhood would bring to his children?

My sister and I both cottoned to Christmas, but truth be told, I liked Chanukah. Looking back, I wonder if this — like so many things that emerged from the sticky soup of growing up — stemmed from my fear. Every night for eight days we lit candles and ate together. My father did not come home late, his little yellow Rabbit pulling into the driveway and screeching to a halt, my mother's crossed arms and wild eyes meeting his fierce whispers, which turned quickly to screams. Chanukah was like tax time, where I was comforted by my father's very presence, his awakeness. I knew he was downstairs trying to make sense of our finances, as I lay awake in the attic, scared of the wicked witch, of beauty's beast, of the ghost of Christmas past, of fire. I could feel the thread that passed between us then, from my scared, prone body down two flights of stairs to my father's seated figure, anxious about what we would have to pay, when each year there was less and less. Chanukah was comforting, and I enjoyed the stories my mother insisted on telling: *This was the oil; this was the fight for freedom. See here? The eternal candle.*

Like the High Holidays, these times felt to me like my mother's days. They tethered me to her, whereas on most every other day, I felt quite far away.

But no matter what, the gifts came on Christmas.

"We need to be open to everything," my father would say. "All cultures."

"Don't you pull that," my mother would say. "We know about all kinds of cultures. Your Christmas is a Hallmark card. Say what you will, but the issue here is not the Jews."

THE JEWS, THE JEWS. There really wasn't much to discuss with the Jews in my class about Chanukah, but come Christmas, I stood with the Christians during homeroom, swapping stories of leaving cookies out for Santa and writing a long note, not just about what we wanted but what the year had been like. The highs and lows, my father would say as he put the plate of Oreos — his favorite — by the fireplace. The embers burned and crackled as my mother hid upstairs, her rage traveling a straight line from her bedroom to the living room, where my father tapped a pen to his head, thinking of what my sister and I should tell Santa. And after we opened our presents on Christmas, I went straight upstairs to call my friends and see what they had gotten from Santa as well.

Here too was connection — me to my father, an unbroken line

strewn with pine needles and candy canes, a cheery connection that in turn connected our family to all the families we saw on television.

FINALLY, WHEN I was eight years old — three years after my sister's birth sent me to the attic — my mother and I walked into the pet store on Wisconsin Avenue on the afternoon of Christmas Eve. This was the store next to the denim and boot shop, where three months earlier, just before I'd started third grade, my mother had made me try on Wranglers and had brought her hand up between my legs. "How's the crotch?" she'd screamed, and I swear to God, she'd yelled it out of the store and onto the street, where young, cool teenagers ate Mexican food beneath the swaying canopy, and into the sky for other countries to hear. I reddened now just walking by the place and into the pet store which was part of that strip on the long, busy stretch of street that connected the District to my neighborhood.

We had been to this pet store many times at my insistence, the least my mother could do after humiliating me to the very heavens. The store smelled like hair and jungle and sawdust and crap, and we were greeted by the warm sound of bubbles rising to the top of aquariums and birds chirping. I went straight to the small-mammal section: hamsters, gerbils, bunnies. And then I saw the guinea pigs. If I could not have a dog, a lovely golden retriever, his bushy tail wagging at my every arrival, this, then, was what I wanted for Chanukah or for Christmas. Not some tiny little smooshable hamster, or a regular bunny like Arnold Rothstein across the street had — a guinea pig seemed exotic, and big enough to put a leash around and walk the block with. A real pet, another heart: company.

I was very excited by my choice; a calico, the clerk, a woman in Birkenstocks, her waist-length white hair streaked with black, described him. Black with bits of orange, some white. I loved the way he felt cupped in both of my hands. I could feel teeth gnawing at my palm.

"Ecch," my mother said, shivering. "I'm sorry, but it's just disgusting."

"I think he's cute." I rubbed my cheek against the guinea pig. "I love him already."

My mother grimaced. "I don't think you should have that in your room," she said.

I looked up at my mother, my eyes filling with tears. "Please!" I said.

"Is it sanitary?" she asked the pet store clerk.

"If you change the cage often enough it is," she said. She smelled of patchouli and sandalwood soap. Smiling beatifically at the animal, she took him from me, placing him carefully back into the store cage.

"I'll do it," I told my mother. "I promise I will!"

"Well, if your room is any indication . . ."

The woman smiled at me and my mother. "I'll hold the guinea pig for you," she said. "Why don't you take a few days to figure out if it's exactly what you want."

"It is!" I said. "It is exactly!" And if I could not have that dog and his big sloppy kisses, I wanted this guinea pig desperately.

"Thank you," my mother said knowingly. "But we would really like the guinea pig."

"To be honest," the clerk said, "we like to protect the animals. And before Christmas, it's just such a chaotic time. I never let them go on Christmas Eve." She rubbed her nose and her silver rings caught the light from the glowing, bubbling aquariums. The guinea pig sucked happily at his water bottle, his tiny teeth clicking against the metal spout.

"Well, not in our house it isn't," my mother said. "We're Jewish."

"Oh," the woman said, considering it. "Well, then it should be fine."

My mother nodded encouragingly. "Really," she said. "Christmas Eve is nothing in our house."

I looked at my mother as she said this and waited for her to elbow me or wink, but she made no move to acknowledge the ruse.

WE PURCHASED THE CAGE, pellets of food, the water bottle, the salt lick, the sawdust, and nothing short of a mini-playground — to the tune of what my mother said, as we drove home along Wisconsin Avenue, was more a year of college than stuff for a hamster.

"Guinea pig, you mean."

"You sure better enjoy it," she said.

"Oh, I will," I said. I held the guinea pig, GP — I'd named him just as we passed Mazza Galleria and the American Café on the way home — in my lap. "I will!" I could feel him nibbling softly on my thighs, his thick, pelletlike body warm on the very crotch my mother had grabbed not three months before when she'd bought these jeans, and I stroked him lovingly.

My father greeted us at the door, a wooden spoon in one hand, for stirring his wine and spices, my sister in the other. "Ooh," he said as I walked by holding GP with two hands. "Couldn't you at least have gotten a rabbit? When I was a kid — "

"Enough about when you were a kid," my mother said.

"It's ugly!" my sister said.

"Is not!" I said.

"Rabbits are trainable, you know," my father said. "They can poop in one little corner of the cage. Once I knew a rabbit who could go to the bathroom on the toilet."

"You did not!" I said.

"Well, I don't think you can train a guinea pig to do much of anything."

"No," said my mother, "I don't think you can."

But I held GP close to my heart and could hear his little one thumping — or was it mine? — as I climbed the stairs to my room. My mother followed, helping me move the record player and set up everything on the little table across from my bed, so that I could see my new pet at night. My father brought my sister up to have a look, and the four of us stood there peering in, waiting for GP to run on his new, bright-silver wheel. When he just sat there, looking out at us with one eye, I pulled him out of his cage for my sister to pet, and she didn't shy away. Then the three of them went downstairs and I lay in bed, my hands clasped behind my head, watching GP rut and drink water and lick from his bar of salt. For the first time in years, it seemed, I felt at ease. I could hear my guinea pig rutting in his sawdust and I didn't feel alone.

That night we did what I once thought all Jews did: we prepared for Christmas. This entailed watching my father make a fire. We all sat before it, and my father passed my mother a hot mug of mulled wine, which she held like a bear between two paws. While GP stirred alone upstairs — *he's tired, sweetie, a lot went on today* — my father read " 'Twas the Night Before Christmas," beneath his Christmas cards and surrounded by a forest of poinsettias. And as the final pièce de résistance, we went to the kitchen to sing songs on the refrigerator.

Christmas carols. On the refrigerator.

My father would lift us up and my sister and I would sing

on top of the refrigerator. I am ashamed to admit how much revolved around that refrigerator — the obvious eating, yes, the picking from leftovers and drinking from cartons, but also drawing with erasable pens, always my father's apology in the form of a shaky young girl's face greeting me and my sister hopefully each morning after nights when he and my mother kept us up with their fighting.

On all other celebratory days, my father placed us on the refrigerator and, as he stood below, looking up to his daughters, we all sang the French national anthem: *Allons enfants de la patrie, Le jour de gloire est arrivé!* We looked out at the kitchen, hands held high to our foreheads like sailors.

That night we did what I once thought all Jews did: we prepared for Christmas.

And tonight, on Jewish Christmas Eve, which wasn't Christmas at all but merely the accoutrements of that holiday, the things that people did on its surface but never what brought them to that surface, not faith or love or a long line of reaching back, not like those days holding our mother's hand on the way to Yom Kippur services to say Kol Nidre, that song so sad and pure it still carries me, nothing serious at all, nothing to hold to, only what we had seen so many people do on television and had read in *A Child's Christmas in Wales*, which was part of my father's ritual on Christmas Day, tonight we sing carols.

I was too big to stand on the fridge and so now I sat, legs dangling to the mustard-colored freezer section as my sister, her hair pulled into blond pigtails, a little gentile, sang "Jingle Bells" on top of the refrigerator at the top of her lungs.

And then, in the lull between songs, my father said, "Let's hang the stockings!"

I remember my mother's angry face, how it turned away from him and from us, to disconnect herself from this tradition she didn't want, that was not ours. And as she turned, my father went to grab her arm, tenderly, to bring her back into the fray of our family, and so he too was turned then when my sister, thrilled to the idea of the stockings and what soon would fill them, walked right off the refrigerator and slammed her chin on the kitchen floor. I watched her from above as her face seemed to explode, facedown, her pigtails sprouting from the back of her head like wilted flowers.

There was screaming and yelling and utter chaos and crying and frantic calls to doctors and hospitals and I remained on top of the refrigerator looking down on it all, remembering our promise, my promise, to the aging hippie at the pet store who let us take my guinea pig because we lied to her and told her that Christmas Eve did not matter to us. Could GP hear the screaming? Was he nervous and scared, did he want to go back to the store?

And I was selfish in that moment, as my mother rushed upstairs and out of her robe and slippers and into her jeans and that green down coat she still wears, and as my father carried my sister down to the garage, in that I did not want to go but wanted, for the first time in my life, to be alone, to be completely separate from them: they are them, I am me. I thought this *then*. Who will care for GP if I leave him there all alone in the attic? What if something is really wrong and we don't come back? He will wake up to nothing, no voices below coming through to him in the dark or dawn, and I knew so well what that would feel like that I fought my father as he came back up from the garage to take me down from the refrigerator. Once down, despite my flailing, I crossed my arms and refused the coat my mother held for me to climb into, until my father raised his voice, pointed that damn finger he would spend his life pointing at me, and dragged me into the Volare, where we sped off into the night to Sibley Memorial Hospital, an emergency room filled with the wreckage of all the miserable individuals Christmas Eve brings, each of them destroyed outside and in by this holiday my father wanted so badly to make his own.

THERE IS NO moral here — as in, this is what happens when you try to be someone you are not. The nurse did call the police, believing my sister's fall to have been not what my parents named it but child abuse. Who puts a child on a refrigerator? My mother stepped up in front of her husband when it was clear that the line of questioning was more than simple procedure.

"This really is not as it seems," I remember her saying over and over again.

My father was angry, but for the first time I saw him rendered unable to show it. "It sounds strange, but it's a tradition we have," he said between clenched teeth.

At the end of it all, my sister was most upset by the socks they put on her hands so that she wouldn't scratch at her stitches — ten of them, in her chin. We had all watched as the doctor sewed her up, her impossibly young face, her eyes fluttering open and closed, as wrecked as my mother's old cracked dolls. We drove back to our house in silence and I, me, because now this story is mine, thought of my guinea pig, and how I had let him down. Forever, I thought, our first night of separateness would come between us.

TWO YEARS LATER we got a dog — a cairn terrier we called Toto, if you can believe it — and GP lost his allure. At my mother's suggestion — *you have to walk and feed and brush Toto now!* — I donated GP to our school, and he lived among the snakes and gerbils as he had in that pet store, which is now a Brazilian restaurant. The denim store is now part of a Whole

Foods. How could that animal have been so important to me one moment, and then the next, nothing?

I can't understand it, as I am now a person who rarely goes anywhere without my own dog, a springer spaniel who I would throw myself in front of a car for, run into that burning building that so terrified me as a child, to save. After that incident, Christmas became more a part of our lives. Perhaps my mother could no longer fight it. Still we lit the candles each Chanukah, but Christmas Day grew larger, to the point where our Jewish relatives would come for what they soon termed Christmakah. There would be ham and glogg and fruitcake: Who didn't want to try on something they had spent their lives outside?

That's what it always felt like: like trying something on. But what was real? I grew more troubled not by Christmas, per se, but by what I would do with it. Out of that childhood, I went on to Brandeis University and then to teach Jewish American literature and to write fiction out of that tradition. Is it some strange Hegelian dialectic? My parents gave me many gifts, but none of them were about being Jewish in the religious sense of the word. Our Jewishness was everything my family was not: it was quiet, celebrated without ceremony, not easily held to.

When I look back at it now, I see it less in the festival of lights, the nights our family was stitched together tipping one candle to another, two equal flames from one, proof that there is always enough — love? light? — to go around, but more in the funerals of my great-grandparents and great-aunts, and then traveling down and down to my grandparents and uncles: a gathering of people, sharing food and memories and, as it grows closer and closer, unbearable grief.

And yet Christmas is part of my family history now. What will it mean for my children, when and if I have them? What will I pass on? Because somewhere in a child's room — mine? — there will be a cabinet, a box, a trunk stashed far back in a closet that will have my mother's terrifying dolls, my father's brushes, stiff with very old paint, and a photograph of my sister and me, holding hands beneath the mistletoe, smiling up at our father, who I'm sure is the one behind the lens.

The Only Dreidel in Idaho

SINCE I GREW UP IN MANHATTAN, THE LAND OF JEWY JEWSTEINS, FELLOW 212'S GASP IN HORROR WHEN I TELL THEM I HAVE SPENT EVERY CHANUKAH SINCE BIRTH IN IDAHO. AS NEW YORK STARTS TO CHOKE ME IN DECEMBER, WITH THRONGS OF FANNY-PACK-WEARING TOURISTS IN SWISH-SWISH SUITS GLUTTING Fifth Avenue, I am always desperate to get to the wide-open Rockies, free of crowds and full of sky. But can you import this treasured Jewish holiday from loxland to landlocked Idaho? I have learned that you can.

Yes, it's true: thirty-one menorah lightings in the capital of potatoes, though no one there has ever heard of a latke. If you mentioned the word, they'd probably think it was a kind of hat or something. Let's face it: the state ain't exactly chock-full o' brethren — that is, unless you're talking about the crazyass skinhead and neo-Nazi compound-dwelling kind. Granted, my fam is hardly in some David Koresh – style arms-bearing militia — we ski in Sun Valley, a century-old resort with old-world glamour that's also heavy on rough-around-the edges rustic charm. But as my friends have often pointed out, if we were to get into our rental car and drive an hour in any direction, we'd be exiting the tiny pocket of blue in a blood-red state: the oversized-sunglass-and-Prada-ski-outfit set from the Hollywood scene would quickly seem far away, the giant Rocky Mountains a symbol of the drastic shift in social and religious spikes.

> **I grew up in Manhattan, the land of Jewy Jewsteins.**

If you Google "Jews" + "Idaho," not surprisingly the top sites are all related to antidefamation or, more horrifyingly, are blogs by various Neanderthals ranting from their log cabins about Anne Frank's diary being a hoax or claiming that 9/11 was, like the Plague, the Depression, and Every Bad Thing Ever, caused by those horned Jews. According to research conducted by Idaho State University professor Jim Aho, potato country is second only to Montana in our fifty states as the worst bastion of radical "Christian patriot" groups, home to countless maniacal factions like the Order, Aryan Nation, and the Tabernacle of Phineas Priesthood, all of whom celebrate Hitler's birthday. You're thinking: Gee, what a great place to light them candles and say Happy Chanukah! *L'chaim*, people!

But despite nearby bonkers mountainfolk, the place has an enchanting charm that keeps calling us back every year, beginning with my dad's first trip as a bachelor with friends over four decades ago. Because I'm so lucky to live in the melting pot of the planet, the capital of the world, the Big Apple, I normally never have any weird moments of self-consciousness about being Jewish. I love my synagogue, frequently weave Yiddish or my mom's Ladino into sentences, talk openly about our Shabbat services or holidays, and have the company of "one in four, maybe more" Jewish peeps on the same twelve-mile isle.

But when I'm in Idaho, I suddenly feel like Woody Allen eating at Annie's WASPy Wisconsin dining table, complete with full Hasidic curlicues. It's not like I ever had Grammy Hall – style face-offs with outward anti-Semites; it's subtler than that. Never has there been an actual run-in with a real-life knuckle-dragging, swastika-tattooed freak show, à la countless Web sites I encountered. But sometimes feeling alien is on a less pronounced level; let's just say a *kippah* in Idaho feels about as common as a jockstrap in a convent. And going from what Jesse Jackson once called "Hymietown" to a place where nary a wall is sans moosehead is a shock to the system.

"Okay, all ten bags are here!" my dad says, counting aloud, as we move our luggage to a corner. I spy a crunchy couple with just the packs on their backs looking at us and can practically feel the eye-roll on deck. We are the East Coast brats who show up at holiday time with all our crap, instead of "keepin' it real" with one duffel. But what can I say? Traveling with kids is not so easy. It's not like I'm bringing extra après-ski outfits and D&G fur-lined moon boots, just some unglam stuffed animals, bottles, formula, and diapers; we need a bunch of things from home to make the transition seamless.

After the endless schlep (which also raises a question from my Jewish friends: Why the haul?) we are finally checked in. Hey, I hate the trek; I wouldn't do it if it wasn't really worth it — but once we unpack and exhale, I feel solar systems away. Gone is the jam-packed gritty island I live on. It's instantly different here. It is stark. It's quiet. It's whiter than white — and not because of the heaps of glittering snow. I'm talking the highest concentration of blonds outside Scandinavia. I am now in the land of quasi-albino Nordic mountainfolk.

"IIIIIII'm dreeeaming of a whiiiiite Christmas," croons Bing Crosby's voice on the hotel lobby speaker. Given our surroundings, those lyrics are a double entendre.

"Merry Christmas!" greets the concierge as we come downstairs for some ho-cho and cookies.

"Look at da Cwishmish twee!" my daughter says, sprinting to

examine the china (and Made in China) ornaments that bedeck the pine.

The East Coast P.C. greeting "Happy Holidays" (cause, huh, what other holiday would there be?) is not heard in these parts. And even in the chic resort town of nearby Ketchum, lawn ornaments featuring Jesus 'n' Co. line the roads, along with rooftop Santas and full sleighs, complete with all eight reindeer and architected stable crèches bigger than many Manhattan apartments. There are Virgins. There are Wise Men. If the soundtrack to a jammed Times Square on New Year's Eve is Frank Sinatra, then the holidays in Idaho seemingly have a constant "Pah-rum-pa-pum-pum" on repeat. The Sun Valley Company, owned by Mormon Earl Holding, employs apple-cheeked carolers to roam the resort singing "O Holy Night" while ringing bells and heralding the Dear Savior's birth. But hey, it is America; I mean, I know every word to every Christmas carol, ain't nothing wrong with that.

Listen, I'll be honest: I love little twinkling lights and the smell of pine trees! Bring on the Ho-ho-ho-ing old dude with prezzies, I can handle that! What is semistrange is that inescapable feeling that we are somehow . . . freaks. There was a time as a kid where, upon spinning an imported East Coast dreidel, I remarked that it was probably the only one spinning in the state at that moment. When you know you are part of a group that is extremely rare, you start to feel a little paranoid, to think that if you scratched the surface of the smiles and mistletoe, you could find someone who loathes the Tribe.

For example, as I listened to the chime-filled songs of the perma-smile octet, I couldn't help but wonder if caroler No. 7 thinks we will burn in the eternal hellfire of Satan's bubbling lava pit of despair and torture for killing that poor tot in the manger.

A platinum blonde steps out of the horseshoe of singers for her solo.

"Santa baby! Just one more teeny little thing," she croons with a bright smile. *"A ring! And I don't mean on the phone . . ."*

Oh, and *we're* the materialistic ones! Just kidding. But seriously, the notion of closet Jewphobia is somewhat confirmed when you peruse some of the local aforementioned blogs. "The Romans did it" obviously ain't being bought (special shout-out of thanks, Mel Gibson!).

And yet we unpack our menorah and blue and white candles in this Charlton Heston–loving place where every single human says "you bet" instead of "yes." I'm not kidding. We all sit down to get lunch after we arrive every year, and we always say we haven't officially settled in Sun Valley till we've heard our first *you bet.*

We are in a rough 'n' tumble western tavern with ceiling-high beer bottles, expired license plates, and taxidermy galore. There is an old pinball machine that eerily harkens back to Jodie Foster in *The Accused*. Females are scarce. Football is on the TV, and flannel abounds. But the blackened-chicken burgers are the best on the planet.

"Can I please get some fries with that?" I ask.

"YOU BET!"

We all grin at one another; the waiter has no clue it's a fam inside joke.

"Oh, and a large Sprite, please?"

"Yoooou BET!"

My husband literally snarfs up his water laughing.

In the evenings, we all gather in my parents' room before going out — my mom corrals us to come and "do Chanukah." We have our family tradition of lighting the candles, singing Chanukah songs, and opening presents my mom has expertly packed with piles of tissue paper, lest the Bloomie's box get damaged en route. The tradition my parents started when we were children is actually semi-Thanksgivingesque, as my brother, husband, mom, dad, and I each take a turn lighting a candle, saying what we are thankful for in that moment.

"Light da pink one!" my daughter requests, as I set the wick aflame when it's my turn.

"I am thankful we are all here together," I say, getting emotional, as my brother lives in Los Angeles.

We pass the candle around the family to light all of them, each person articulating their gratitude: how blessed to be able to be healthy, to have kids, and even just to travel. In a resort town, everyone is high on life; it's a special time of feeing alive and refreshed, leaving the stress of "real life" behind.

There is a soothing calm to the placid pace. No one's in any big rush. Natch, this does suck when you literally wait twenty minutes after asking what the soup du jour is only to have the waitress return to tell you it's "the soup of the day!" But bratty New Yorker impatience aside, the mellowed meter is in sync with what I want Chanukah to be — enjoyed not in a fierce frenzy but as a slow time where you can drink in the flickering candles and actually have time to watch them burn down. The wax spills over onto the tray, and my fastidious mom always starts scraping it away with an expired credit card so as to have the slate clean for the next night, while all of us go, "Mom, please! Sit! Stop scraping!"

Because New York is so far away — two plane rides and often a two-hour bus trip from Twin Falls, thanks to an airport that is shut half the time — our friends are mostly West Coasters. One family from L.A. became our add-water-and-stir insta-pals — because they were Jewish, there was a natural click, as if we were part of a club that, perched in the Intermountain West, has very few members. But this year I learned that there are more than I thought. With my Googling fingers at the ready, I did some research.

Shocker of all shockers, the first Jewish governor in the United

States was elected in . . . Idaho! Swear. Moses Alexander, in 1914. To say I was floored at this discovery is not an understatement. I literally had to be spatulaed off the carpet. Next I found that the oldest synagogue west of the Mississippi is in Boise! Ahavath Beth Israel, founded in 1895! Jaw-on-sisal. While the best guesstimates still put the statewide Jewish population at under a few thousand,

> **Shocker of all shockers, the first Jewish governor in the United States was elected in . . . Idaho! Swear.**

I was elated to find that we weren't the only ones crackin' out the menorah by a long shot. I used to always feel very former Soviet Union with our secret lighting, wondering if the housekeeping staff in our hotel walked in and saw our holiday corner they'd think we were doing some peculiar cult ritual in our perky hotel room, which was decorated in cheery peachy colors, not unlike a tampon box.

As a child, when the holidays fell on the earlier side (try explaining the schizo nature of Chanukah calendar placement to a confused Christian sometime), we would celebrate in New York. Sometimes it would be for a few days and then we'd celebrate the rest in Idaho; sometimes it would be one night. Aside from the psychological difference between toasting the festival o' lights in a place with millions of Jews and doing it in a place with seemingly zero, our whole ambience could not have been more distinct.

There are no synagogues in Sun Valley. When we were in New York, we'd go to our temple, and the religious-school children (*moi* from grades two through seven) would light candles and sing songs as familiar faces packing the pews looked on. Our temple, Central Synagogue, on Fifty-fifth Street, is the most beautiful, majestic place in the world — just the space is enough to make you feel humble and religious, and upon entering I have always felt in the presence of something amazing. (Funnily enough, the other equally humbling sight is the endless view of the mountains at the top of Baldy in Idaho.)

Then there's my temple's close-knit community — warm and caring, our interactions always accompanied by music. The services always call on everyone to introduce themselves to their neighbors in the pews, so that should people enter alone they will not leave as strangers. The enormous room with the soaring ceiling always felt accessible and even cozy, with the lights turned down and only the flicker of candlelight to ring in the holidays.

Back at home in our apartment, we would gather in the living room for our own mini-service and present opening. We had my mother's antique silver menorah — it's a Sephardic heirloom that is hundreds of years old. It feels linked to the past, to the traditions of all the family members who lit it before. It lived shrouded in blue felt, and I saw its zippered special case throughout the year as I rummaged to steal a piece of chocolate from my mom's candy stash, which lived in the same small hall closet. Aside from boxed confections brought by guests, this closet housed the familiar blue boxes of candles (the box all American Jews would recognize, without a graphic design spruce-up in over thirty years) as well as other Judaica pieces: kiddush cups, prayer books, special plates, and piles of our family-friendly Haggadahs, which yield a Seder that does not exceed thirty minutes. Which my family lovingly calls McSeder.

But our Sun Valley menorah is what we call our travel menorah — it came from Gracious Home and literally has a $14.99 sticker on it, which doesn't feel too holy, though somehow, when we are gathered around it, none of that matters. Even with our tacky menorah, which was probably made somewhere in Asia, where there are even fewer Jews than Idaho, it's the soul of family together that makes the holiday — not our menorah or our synagogue. In fact, now Chanukah is so synonymous with our brightly hued hotel room in Sun Valley that I don't even miss not being in sanctuary at home; *this* is what the holidays are to me and to my family.

"Chanukah, oh Chanukah, come light the menorah! Let's have a party, we'll all dance the horah!" we sing.

We're not literally dancing in a circle in our hotel room — though I think we did as little kids — but it's fun to still sing the songs and rock it ol' skoo.

So where does a holiday exist? Sure, there are familiar trappings of a service or the rituals, but I then thought about how many Jews through history had to import their holidays with them, without even a candle to light, let alone a place to worship or safely open a prayer book. They brought the holidays with them inside their souls, and that would always be their sanctuary as they drew from the vault of their memories. So Idaho, with its cold piles of snow and low head count of Torah-toting brethren, was barely a challenge. We brought on the whole "we are the only Jews here" ourselves — because it is in America, we always knew we were free to do what we wanted, which has always made it safe and comforting to us, even with raised eyebrows from the blond room service guy who, with arched brow, surveys our Chanukah accoutrements on the side table.

One year, after a dry spell from temple (I guiltily hadn't been since the High Holy Days and never wanted to be a "twice a year" Jew), I was missing that warm, cozy feeling of songs and candles and, not to be cheesy, a "holy space." At our friends' annual Christmas Eve party, a bunch of people were talking about going to a nearby midnight Mass. The local church is called (swear to G dash D) Our Lady of the Snow. Seriously. Everyone started talking about how the songs are so spine-tinglingly beautiful with the velvety airtight harmonies and the adorable children who line the aisles with candles.

"Jill, come with us!" a pal invited when I remarked how nice it sounded.

Fifteen people were all headed over shortly and gushed about what a stunning, memorable service it would be. Because the picture they painted was so soothing, triggering calming visions of my own synagogue, I decided to go too. And memorable it was indeed.

The service is burned in my brain indelibly, not because I was into it but because of the humiliating gut-churning shizzle that went down. Just when I had been feeling all Zen about being a Jewish person in Idaho, I entered the church. I didn't immediately feel uncomfortable, though the whole nails-in-wrists crucifix thing has always creeped me out a little, and the people all seemed to be wearing knitted Christmas sweaters with yarn reindeer or wreaths affixed to them. It was a sea of red and white turtlenecks, shining cross necklaces, and smocked-dress-wearing blond children. But like I said, as an American I know and love those Christmas songs, so I looked around and hoped the singing would begin soon. There ended up being some songs— but they were more hymnlike in nature than "Winter Wonderland." And then came the doozy. The priest got up and did his sermon and droned on and on, and just as I was starting to drift from paying attention— it was two A.M. New York time, after all— he astounded me. He was talking about something in the Bible where there was a new tax levied.

"The Jews were all upset about paying more," he bemoaned. "Some things never change!"

There was a ripple of laughter through the church. I froze. My whole row, which was populated by our family's friends, also didn't budge. Slowly, as I simply stared straight forward unblinking, one girl leaned down cautiously to gauge my reaction. I even saw out of the corner of my eye another friend nudge her husband. Suddenly it went from potentially nice heartwarming carol-and-candle night to sinister snickerfest about them greedy Jews. What upset me the most, though, was the dumb smile on the priest's face — he felt like he was in on some big inside joke, knowing everyone would laugh like that. I felt as if a laser beam was shining on me, thrusting me back into Hasidic mode; it was so cringe-inducing I wanted to bolt, for fear a Dr. Evil button would be pushed and my pew would suck me down into a fiery abyss. I swallowed hard, not even acknowledging my pals' attempts at a facial apology on behalf of their assholic clergy, and I stuck it out until the end of the Mass. At the finish, there were candles held by children, but the would-be tender image suddenly felt cold and remote. I couldn't wait to go home and report the sitch to my parents.

I guess I had expected stuff like that from hicks in the sticks hours away, but not in the cozy resort town I loved and certainly not from a leader of that generally kind community. I was so incensed I haven't gone into a church since, and while obviously not all churches are Our Lady of the Snow, I started having the sneaking feeling that that kind of sermon occurred often and in far more incendiary decibels than I'd experienced. That was seven years ago. I've since adored returning every year and relish that time away, but I must admit I never pass that church without remembering the experience. The current me would have stormed up to the priest after and blasted him, but I was in a vulnerable post-breakup

I met and married an NJB.

state then, exhausted and in shock. Yet going through that strengthened me. See, I wasn't always Super-Jew.

My brother, who has blond hair and blue eyes, has often been mistaken for a gentile, and more than a few times he's overheard various slurs against Jews, spoken by people never suspecting he was Jewish. I, on the other hand, look more stereotypically like a Jewess, so I never heard any weird remarks of that nature. And while I was dragged kicking and screaming to Sunday school, my brother excitedly went and flourished — he even wore a star of David, which at the time I found a tad excessive. But things slowly changed after the whole midnight Mass thing — and a failed relationship with a gentile guy whose mom, in trying to bond with me, said, "Guess what?! We went and rented *Schindler's List* last night!"

Through the years, I got stronger and stronger with respect to the importance of my Jewish identity, and after dating scores of reversible-names *Mayflower* people (example: Rutherford Wellington could be Wellington Rutherford. Doesn't quite work with Abramowitz Ari, does it?), I met and married an NJB, a nice Jewish boy. He loves our time in Idaho and loves spending Chanukah there every year.

And now that we have children of our own, I realize the importance of these traditions as building blocks for who they are. My daughter Sadie, who somehow flukishly got my brother's recessive coloring, which blends in more with homogenized Pacific Northwest than melting-pot Manhattan, will in all likelihood be exposed to the same subtle riffing my brother endured. And I need to make sure she is strong enough to deal with it. A good start is by creating firm touchstones like my parents did — patterned experiences that will always help her return to her family and, ultimately, to herself: yearly moments filled with songs and light and love, like our family made in Sun Valley, a place with firm traditions that honed and strengthened our identity even further than our New York roots by taking them and transplanting them far away in our little family nest perched in nowheresville. So what if our little blue and white candles feel rare — *we* make our own temple in our closeness and warmth, our teeny snow-kissed congregation of seven, and that nearness means more than any yarmulke head count.

Rock of Ages

EVERY CHANUKAH, THE CHOIR AT MY JEWISH DAY SCHOOL PERFORMED TWICE: ONCE AT THE SCHOOL'S ANNUAL CHANUKAH CELEBRATION, AND THEN THE NEXT DAY AT THE NEIGHBORHOOD'S LOCAL PUBLIC SCHOOL, TO BRING A LITTLE CHANUKAH SPIRIT TO "LOST" JEWISH KIDS WHO WERE INUNDATED WITH CHRISTMAS MARKETING AND KNEW NOTHING about the miracle of Chanukah but were more than happy to tolerate our singing if it meant missing some class. Our choir was composed of about thirty girls and twelve boys from the sixth through eighth grades.

Fact: Most kids possessed of a functioning set of testicles did not join the choir.

But I did, for the same reason that boys and men have always done stupid things: because of a girl. There were eleven other boys in the choir, and while I never confirmed it, it's a safe bet that they were all similarly motivated. Except for this kid named Aaron Berkowitz, who could sing in a high, prepubescent mezzo-soprano that brought tears to the eyes of anyone over sixty, and whom we made fun of mercilessly because, as a general rule, mezzo-sopranos fight like girls. Also my friend Joey Weitz, who years later, to no one's great surprise, would be the first member of our grade to officially come out. Joey's voice had already begun to change, it squeaked like Peter Brady when he sang, and he knew it. He had joined to be ironic. But I have to believe that the rest of the boys, like me, were in it for the girls. Where else but at choir practice could an acutely shy, libidinous kid like me stand shoulder to shoulder, swaying as one, with thirty of the better-looking girls in the school, joined with them into a single musical orifice, united under our common objective of singing complicated Israeli songs in three-part harmony and not sucking? It was the closest I would come to sex for quite some time.

The girl was Tara Wahlberg. She was a year older, already in eighth grade, but she had a learning disability that put her in some of my seventh-grade classes. I thought it was cool that she had a learning disability, a sexy bit of damage, like a butterfly tattoo. When a woman is out of your league, she has to be damaged in some way for there to be any hope. Tara had short, messy blond hair that she was growing out from last year's ill-advised pixie cut, intense brown eyes, and full, frowning lips that parted provocatively when she sang. Her voice was nothing special, was actually a little shrill, but she could carry a tune and she sang with no fear, and thus was awarded solos regularly.

When she sang, I would watch the rushed expansions of her back ribs through her polo shirt as she took her breaths, and the soft, liquid flex of the calf muscles under her skin as she rocked ever so slightly from side to side. When you're twelve years old, that's really all it takes, some small, unarticulated aspect of beauty you can excavate

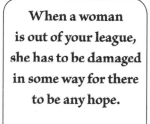

When a woman is out of your league, she has to be damaged in some way for there to be any hope.

like a secret and call your own. Tara had smooth, well-formed calves and those full, creased lips, and I was in love, and you don't need any better proof than the fact that I was willing to stay after school every Tuesday to be subjected to the steady abuse of our fat, sweaty choir director, simply to be in the same room as Tara.

Our choir director was a fearsome Israeli of accomplished girth whose name I don't dare write even today, but suffice it to say that it lent itself quite handily to the nickname "Cockman," which all the boys called him behind his sweat-stained back. His temperamental outbursts were rendered more sinister by his thick Sabra accent, and the sweaty patches of scalp seen through his thinning curly hair gleamed like polished marble under the stage lights. But there was no denying Cock-man's talent, his ability to simultaneously sing all three parts of the harmony while banging on the piano keys and shouting at us that we were idiots (pronounced *eed-yots*). The guy could multitask. He smelled of sour chickpeas and body odor and was known from time to time, when he was particularly irked, to violently hurl the red banquet chairs we sat on across the room. These outbursts seemed to be reserved exclusively for the boys in the choir, and we were all a little terrified of Cock-man, but love made us bold and so we soldiered on.

Whenever the choir was slated to perform, we would be excused from classes for extra rehearsals. So Chanukah, with two major performances, was a bonanza, two entire afternoons spent out of class, in the close confines of the music theater — just Tara, me, and forty other kids. And as we practiced the various numbers relating to the miracle of Chanukah, I fantasized about my own miracle, a carefully crafted sequence of events that culminated in Tara's kissing me with those soft, frowning lips for a very long time. Usually this involved terrorists of unknown origin and purpose taking over the school and me utilizing my advanced-green-belt karate skills to save her, resulting in said kiss. Other times it was as simple as finding her crying in the dark hall that, for reasons I've never understood, ran between the boys' and girls' bathrooms behind the stage. That was the make-out spot of choice in our school, or so I'd heard, and in my fantasy I found her there alone, crying about her broken family and her learning disability. I would comfort her, and she would put her head on my shoulder, and then she would turn her face up to mine and, sensing my hesitation, which would be cute and appealing to her, she would put her hands on the sides of my face and guide me in to her moist, parted lips for a prolonged kiss.

Fact: It takes some doing to hide an erection while standing upright in the bass section during choir practice.

It probably doesn't speak well for my self-esteem that, even in my fantasies, I could only ever envision someone wanting to kiss me under extreme emotional duress, but I should tell you that there had been some precedent. We had performed at the school's annual scholarship dinner at the Waldorf-Astoria a month earlier, and since we would have a few hours to kill in an empty banquet room before we went on, the school had arranged for a projector and a screening of *Superman: The Movie*. Through a series of carefully executed maneuvers, I ended up sitting Indian style on the floor next to Tara, and when she shifted position her bare right knee rested easily in the crook of my thigh, just below the hip. We fit together perfectly, and even when my leg fell asleep I didn't dare move, for fear that our contact would be lost, like a distant radio signal. And then, when Margot Kidder fell out of the helicopter, Tara gasped, and when she gasped, she grabbed my arm and squeezed it. Like it was hers to grab. Like she could grab it anytime she wanted to, because we were tight like that.

So you see, headway had, in fact, been made.

This year we would be singing two songs new to our repertoire. A mid-tempo, modern rendition of the traditional Chanukah song "Maoz Tzur" (Rock of Ages), and a complex Hebrew song extracted from the liturgy called "Al Ha-Nissim" (On the Miracles). The "Maoz Tzur" arrangement called for a duet with a male and female singer, and when Cock-man asked for a girl, about twenty hands flew up. After a few quick tryouts, Tara landed the job, and stepped confidently into the bend of the grand piano, the accepted spot for rehearsing soloists. Then Cock-man asked for a male soloist. The only volunteers were Aaron Berkowitz, who already had three solos in the performance, and Joey Weitz, whose eyes twinkled with glee at the thought of mangling the song in front of a full auditorium. Cock-man frowned at the room, clearly displeased with his choices, and I knew this was my chance. If I raised my hand, I was a shoo-in to sing with Tara. It would mean staying late for private rehearsals, and we would be linked, however briefly, as singing partners. But even though I secretly thought I was a pretty decent singer, the prospect of singing alone had always terrified me. Only after Joey Weitz had taken his place next to Tara by the piano did I feel my hand slowly, inconspicuously rise to shoulder height and then quickly fall, the ghost of a braver version of myself who would show up from time to time but never seemed inclined to stick around.

And so we all sat quietly while Joey and Tara learned their solos, Tara staring into space as she sang, Joey belting out his squeaky rasps on key with a comic earnestness no teacher would dare call him out on, and me hating myself for being a coward in matters of the heart.

ON THE FIRST day of Chanukah, all the members of the choir came to school wearing blue and white, the national colors of Israel and the standard uniform of every Jewish day school choir under the sun. White polo shirts and navy slacks for the boys, navy or denim skirts for the girls. Tara surprised me by wearing a formal white blouse, opened at the neck to showcase a wide expanse of porcelain skin and sheer enough that, in the right light, you could make out the tantalizing outline of her bra and the twin bulbs of her emerging breasts. That shirt was a revolution, was its own little Chanukah miracle.

That day we performed before five hundred students and teachers during the school's afternoon Chanukah assembly, and halfway through Joey and Tara's solo, Joey forgot the words. Rather than fall silent, he began to sing "La la la" along with the melody, grinning as the guffaws spread like a wave across the auditorium. Anyone else would have been embarrassed, but Joey just cranked up his faux earnestness a few notches, really projecting his scratchy, pubescent *La*'s to the cheap seats. Not so Tara, who was clearly mortified. Her body tensed up and her voice suddenly wavered as she turned a pleading eye toward Cock-man, who looked ready to stand up and hurl his grand piano at Joey.

The moment the curtain came down, Tara fled backstage to the girls' bathroom, face red, eyes wet. I felt bad for her, but also undeniably aroused. In my dreams, those were the tears that led to our kiss. Tara Wahlberg crying in the girls' bathroom was nothing less than foreplay. So as Cock-man stormed the stage like it was the beach at Normandy, screaming accented bloody murder at Joey Weitz, I slipped off the stage, and then into that inexplicable dark hallway that ran behind the auditorium connecting the two bathrooms.

And there she was, my lovely, damaged Tara in her miraculous shirt, standing against the wall, weeping. But what I had failed to account for in my fantasy is the way in which eighth-grade girls are drawn like moths to melodrama. There had to be at least five other girls standing in a circle around her, rubbing her back, handing her tissues, whispering irately to one another, or just kind of looking on, waiting for some unknowable feminine call to action. When I stepped into the hall from the boys' bathroom, they all turned as one to look at me, and it felt like one of those movies where the white guy wanders into the black bar and the band stops playing and everyone just looks at him, wondering what fart in the cosmos has brought him to this unlikely place. These were eighth-grade girls and I was a seventh-grade boy, which made me something other than a legitimate human, so I wilted under their stares and crumbled into an insubstantial pile of sawdust.

Tara Wahlberg crying in the girls' bathroom was nothing less than foreplay.

Back on the stage, Cock-man was still screaming at Jocy while the rest of the choir stood by, gleefully stupefied. "You don't deserve solo you eed-yot! You don't even deserve this choir!" Cock-man shouted at him.

"It was a mistake," Joey said, admirably keeping his cool in the face of Cock-man's whirling, sweat-soaked rage.

"I make a mistake and kick your head!" This was 1981, when a teacher could say something like that without making the evening news.

"I don't see what the big deal is."

"Get off my choir!" Cock-man screamed, the vein in his forehead writhing like a serpent.

"I'm not standing on it!"

"You get out, now!"

And thus was Joey Weitz kicked off the choir. Cock-man sat

down on his sagging piano bench and pulled out the crumpled, yellowed handkerchief he'd been using for the last decade or so to wipe his prodigiously sweating brow. "Now," he said, rubbing his temples with thick, sausage fingers, "who will sing with Tara?"

And only after I noticed everybody looking at me kind of funny did I fully understand that I had raised my hand, which just goes to show you what the right shirt on a woman will do.

THUS, MY TWELFTH Chanukah brought me a twofold miracle: my singing debut and proximity to Tara Wahlberg. Because, you see, I really did think I could sing. I sang in the shower, I sang in my bed, I sang pretty much anywhere I knew no one could hear me. I sang Billy Joel, Elton John, the Beatles, Bruce Springsteen. I knew, with the unshakable conviction of a twelve-year-old, that, in a pinch, I could step in to front the Electric Light Orchestra or play Danny Zuko in *Grease*. I was destined to be a star. All I needed was the right venue to unleash my talent on the world.

Fact: Many contemporary male novelists really wanted to be rock stars. You will find that we are suspiciously well versed when it comes to rock music. We can rattle off detailed histories of our favorite bands and singers, quote an insane amount of lyrics by heart, discuss the chord structures, list the many times we've seen them in concert, and scribble a list of their essential albums with no forethought at all. Many of us play instruments.

Read McInerney, read Ellis, read Hornby, read King, read Rushdie and countless others, and you'll find enough failed rock stars to people a thousand reality shows. We spent a good deal of our childhoods picturing ourselves onstage in a sold-out arena, singing our heart out for twenty-five thousand screaming fans, or sitting for an interview dressed in funky, rock-star clothes, or going to bed every night in hotel suites with sexy, scantily clad groupies who were more than happy to give it up in the name of rock and roll.

> **I knew, with the unshakable conviction of a twelve-year-old, that, in a pinch, I could step in to front the Electric Light Orchestra or play Danny Zuko in *Grease.***
>
> ⮑

Fact: Most of us turned out not to be any good, which is why I was invited to write this story and not to do some blow off Kate Moss's naked ass.

COCK-MAN KEPT THE choir through all of our afternoon classes to rehearse, and spent a good deal of time on the "Maoz Tzur," so that Tara and I could work it out. It shouldn't have been difficult for me, since my part was the same melody line I'd been singing with the group, but now, no longer able to disappear into the collective voice of the choir, my voice sounded thin and shaky to me, and singing out loud felt like the dream where you show up to school without your pants. Also,

Tara's part was in a minor key a few steps higher, and when she sang I was at risk of falling off the precarious perch of my own key. Standing there beside Tara, I was overwhelmed by a potent combination of stage fright and lust, and my chest quivered every time I opened my mouth.

When Cock-man dismissed the choir, he asked if Tara and I would stay behind to practice a little more. He was concerned with our timing, with the blending of our voices. He was concerned that I might suck.

"I can stay," Tara said, looking hopefully at me. She didn't know me well, probably didn't know much more than my name and that I was a seventh grader who lived about a mile away from her, where the houses got bigger, but when she turned those big eyes on me, I would have sworn she knew everything there was to know about me. It was December, when night falls shortly after lunchtime, and staying late would mean walking the six long, uphill blocks to the city bus stop with Tara, alone in the dark, just the two of us, basking in the green-and-amber glow of the Christmas lights wrapped around trees and lining the roofs of houses throughout the neighborhood. We would no doubt get to talking, and she would see that I was a good guy, funny and sincere, quietly cool. Maybe our elbows would bump lightly as we walked, and we would shiver instinctively against each other for warmth. Maybe she would talk about how mortified she'd been when Joey ruined their solo, maybe even crying again at the recollection, and I would pull my glove off to tenderly brush away her tears with my fingers before they froze on her pale, freckled skin. After that, I'd never again be the insignificant seventh grader, just a part of the random human clutter of her day school experience. I'd be the guy she sang a solo with, who wiped her tears away and made her laugh on a cold December evening.

"I can stay," I said.

Tara smiled, and inside me cymbals clashed as the marching band strutted triumphantly down Main Street.

And so we stayed, for an extra hour, and in the privacy of the empty stage my confidence grew. I sang along with more authority, easily staying on key, and every time Tara smiled her approval, I felt a warm tremor in my loins. During a break, when Cock-man left to make a call, I sat down at the piano and absently started to play "Heart and Soul," and after a minute she sat down beside me to play the high part, doing a bluesy little improvisation on the black keys.

"You're good," she said, giggling as I changed tempo.

"So are you," I said.

"I'm doing the easy part."

Her thigh was pressed against mine on the piano bench, our shoulders brushing lightly as we played, and I could smell her scents, lavender, coconut, and wild cherry Bubble Yum. I kept waiting for her to get bored and stop, but she kept right on playing, matching my tempo changes, leaning against me when she giggled. When I jokingly started playing too fast for her, she grabbed my hands with her own and held them prisoner for a second or two, and our heads bumped lightly. I know now that that was the moment I should have kissed her, that that was my window, and it closed as quickly as it had opened, like so many more windows would open and close with other girls in the coming years. But back then, all I knew was that I didn't want the moment to end, and for the twenty minutes or so that we were alone at that piano, Tara Wahlberg was mine, and mine alone. Then Cock-man came back to take us through it one more time, and we stopped abruptly, right in the middle, because everyone knows how to play "Heart and Soul," but no one really knows how to end it.

When we stepped outside it had started to snow, like in a Christmas movie, which meant our walk up to the bus stop would be slower and even more romantic, but then Cock-man pulled up in his battered, puke-green Nova and told us he would drive us home. The car stank of Cock-man's imported body odor. Tara sat up front with him, and when he dropped her off, she called over her shoulder to me, "See you tomorrow," and disappeared into the gathering snow, leaving me desolate and deflated in the back of the reeking Nova. Adding insult to injury, Cock-man made me sing my part for the duration of the drive.

THE NEXT AFTERNOON, right after lunch, we boarded the school bus that would take us to P.S. 141. I thought that maybe I'd save a seat for Tara, but by the time I got on she was already sitting in the back with a group of eighth-grade girls, and even though I looked back there repeatedly on the short ride, we never made eye contact.

The auditorium at P.S. 141 was the real deal. It was at least three times the size of the one at our school, which was really just a gym with a stage when you got right down to it, and it had theater seats on an incline and a professional sound system. By the time we arrived, the place was already filled to noisy capacity with an endless array of long-haired kids in jeans and T-shirts, two wardrobe items expressly forbidden in our school's dress code. Girls were sitting on boys' laps, kids were chewing gum and being rowdy and running down the aisles, and up on that giant stage, in our blue-and-white outfits and with our private school sensibilities, it felt no different to us than playing a gig at Folsom Prison. I was instantly self-conscious about my blue day school yarmulke, my parochial education, and my pleated navy pants.

When the time came for me to step forward and join Tara at the solo mikes, about halfway through the show, I was on the verge of a minor nervous breakdown. As I looked out at the crowd, I could feel my left thigh shaking uncontrollably, the small network of muscles in my cheeks twitching nervously, and I imagined that every soul in that cavernous room could see it too. And then the choir fell silent and next to me Tara took a deep breath and opened her mouth.

I don't remember very much after that. I don't exactly recall singing, but I remember hearing my voice floating back across the auditorium at me from the overhead speaker, thin and hollow and much too flat, not at all how I heard it in my head. I wondered if something might be wrong with the sound system. Tara swayed delicately beside me, staring heavenward as she sang, and I remember feeling intimately connected to her. And the last thing I remember, after our solo was over, was watching Tara slip back into the alto section with nary a look back at me, to be swallowed up into the blue-and-white tapestry of the choir.

I never sang another solo after that. And I never again spent any time with Tara. The social currents of junior high school swept us out to sea on our separate, preordained tides, and while I always kept an eye out for her, and she always said hi to me at choir practice, that was pretty much it. She graduated at the end of the year, and I never saw her again. In the words of the immortal Bruce Springsteen: Love's like that, sure it is.

EVERY YEAR NOW, I still light the candles on Chanukah, which makes me, if nothing else, a Jewish day school success story. And when I light them, I can't help but think of Tara Wahlberg. I wonder what became of her, if she still lights Chanukah candles wherever she is, and if, maybe, she remembers me when she does. The miracle of Chanukah was that a paltry amount of oil in a darkened temple burned in the menorah for eight days. For me, twenty minutes of a winter night in an empty room of a darkened school, sharing a piano bench

> **I still light the candles on Chanukah, which makes me, if nothing else, a Jewish day school success story.**

with a pretty girl, has lasted twenty-five years. There are miracles and there are miracles. Love's like that, sure it is.

I still play a pretty mean "Heart and Soul," by the way. And I still have yet to figure out how it ends.

WHILE MY SUITEMATES FRENZIED ABOUT, STUFFING DIRTY LAUNDRY IN DUFFEL BAGS AND NEGOTIATING RIDE SHARES TO NEW JERSEY, I SAT AROUND IN FLANNELS (IT WAS A TYPICALLY RAW 33 DEGREES IN MEDFORD) AND READ MARGARET ATWOOD...

TOMMY'S AND MY BEST FRIEND, ERIC, WAS OVER. IN OUR FUCKED UP, TRIANGULAR WAY, ERIC, WHO I WASN'T SLEEPING WITH, FELT GUILTY FOR LEAVING ME TO GO SKIING WITH TOMMY, WHO I WAS SLEEPING WITH AND WHO WASN'T FEELING GUILTY AT ALL.

ERIC WAS IN LOVE WITH TOMMY, THOUGH HE SOMEHOW DIDN'T GET THAT TOMMY, ME & THE REST OF THE UNIVERSE KNEW THIS. SO I KNEW THAT AT LEAST PART OF ERIC WAS ECSTATIC AT THE PROSPECT OF A LONG CAR RIDE UP TO VERMONT.

I DIDN'T LOVE TOMMY, BUT I HADN'T YET WEANED MYSELF FROM LOVING GOING OUT WITH HIM. HE WAS HANDSOME AND FUN AND CHARISMATIC.

EVERYONE IN THE ROOM--WHATEVER ROOM--WANTED TO BE TALKING TO TOMMY--TO HAVE TOMMY'S ATTENTION. AND FOR WHATEVER REASON, TOMMY ONLY WANTED MY ATTENTION. AT LEAST MY BODY'S ATTENTION...

FOR THE PAST SEMESTER OF OUR JUNIOR YEAR, WE'D MOSTLY JUST HAD A LOT OF SEX IN HIS SHAMBLES OF A ROOM OFF CAMPUS, THEN MET UP WITH ERIC FOR DINNER AT THE DINING HALL.

ANYWAY, THE PLAN WAS FOR THE TWO OF THEM AND SOME OF THEIR FRIENDS TO HAVE A GUY'S SKI WEEK, AND THEN TO REJOIN ME AT SCHOOL FOR THE DURATION OF THE BREAK, WHERE WE'D GO BACK AND FORTH BETWEEN MY DORM AND THE RATTY TRIPLE-DECKER THAT TOMMY AND ERIC AND 4 OTHER GUYS SHARED IN TEELE SQUARE.

MY WEEKEND WAS LONG AND QUIET AND SORTA BLISSFUL AFTER THE HUBBUB OF FINALS. IT WAS NASTY OUT, SO I MOSTLY ATE CUP O' NOODLES & READ. I'D BEEN TAKING SOMETHING FOR A YEAST INFECTION. IT WASN'T REALLY BOTHERING ME, BUT STAYING IN WAS NICE...

MOM CALLED TO TELL ME THAT SHE'D SENT CHANUKAH GIFTS AND A MENORAH AND THAT EVEN THOUGH SHE AND DAD KNEW THE CRUISE WOULD BE NICE, THEY WERE REGRETTING THE DECISION WE'D ALL MADE AT THANKSGIVING TO GO OUR SEPARATE WAYS THIS WEEK.

...SO I LEFT WITHOUT THE CARE PACKAGE FROM MOM...

JEEZ HOPE THEY AREN'T SENDING FOOD OR MEDS THROUGH THIS JOINT

UNIVERSITY SHIPPING & RECEIVING

THERE WASN'T MUCH TO DO OR BUY IN THE RUNTY MEDFORD NEIGHBORHOOD JUST BEYOND THE UNIVERSITY'S GATES. THIS WAS MASSACHUSETTS AFTER SHOES AND TEXTILES, BEFORE COMPUTERS. THE PLACE HAD BEEN DEPRESSED FOR A HUNDRED YEARS...

I DID STOP IN HILLSIDE SPA TO GET MORE CUP O' NOODLES. PEPE, THE HANDSOME, ITALIAN SON OF THE OWNER, WAS CONCERNED...

Hillside Spa

THE LOTTERY

Drink HOOD Milk

TRUTH BE TOLD, I HAD A LITTLE TROUBLE FOCUSING WHENEVER CONFRONTED WITH A UNIVERSITY BULLETIN BOARD...

HOW COME YOU'RE UP THERE IF THE DORM'S CLOSED?

RESIDENT ASSISTANTS ARE ALLOWED TO STAY.

WELL WHAT AM I SUPPOSED TO DO? SLEEP OUT HERE ON THE PATIO IN THE DRIZZLE?

OK, I CAN LET YOU IN—BUT JUST TO PACK & USE THE PAYPHONE TO MAKE ARRANGEMENTS. YOU'LL HAVE TO LEAVE TOMORROW.

FINE, RIGHT, WHATEVER, DORM STAFF BROWNSHIRT.

SO THE CALL TO TOMMY DIDN'T GO VERY WELL. I TRIED MAKING HIM FEEL GUILTY BY MENTIONING HAVING MISSED MY MOM'S CHANUKAH PRESENT...BUT THAT WAS ONLY GONNA GET ME SO FAR WITH HIM. TOMMY'S THE KIND OF JEW WHO THINKS MACCABEES ARE THE FANCY NUTS PEOPLE BRING BACK FROM THEIR HAWAIIAN VACATIONS.

THERE WAS NO POWER IN MY ROOM WHEN I GOT BACK. IT WAS FREEZING. I GOT UNDER THE COVERS. I WAS PISSED AT TOMMY FOR BEING A SELFISH BASTARD. PISSED AT ERIC FOR FOLLOWING TOMMY AROUND LIKE A TOY POODLE. PISSED AT MY FAMILY FOR GOING ON A CRUISE. PISSED AT MYSELF FOR NOT READING IMPORTANT UNIVERSITY NOTICES. PISSED AT MARGARET ATWOOD BECAUSE I COULDN'T READ HER IN THE DARK.

I DIDN'T KNOW THE ANSWER TO HER QUESTION. EVEN NOW, THOUGH, 20 SOME YEARS LATER, I CAN BE SITTING IN A DOCTOR'S WAITING ROOM OR PUSHING THROUGH AN AIRPORT AND IT WILL OCCUR TO ME THAT I HAVEN'T TALKED TO MY HUSBAND OR MOTHER OR 3 KIDS IN HALF A DAY AND I'LL BE STRUCK WITH THE FACT THAT NO MATTER HOW RICHLY PEOPLED AND CONNECTED MY LIFE IS, IT'S A MODERN LIFE—I'M A BUSINESSWOMAN— A SUCCESSFUL ONE—AND THAT MUCH OF IT, MORE THAN I REALIZE MOMENT TO MOMENT, IS SPENT APART FROM THOSE I LOVE...

SHE WAS BACK IN A FEW HOURS, HOWEVER, AND SHE WASN'T TAKING NO FOR AN ANSWER.

COME USE THE PHONE IN MY APARTMENT. YOU CAN REIMBURSE ME WHEN I GET THE BILL..

HER SINGLE WAS VERY NEAT AND SPARE. BOSTON CELTICS CLOCK RADIO BY THE BED. A SHELF OF AFRICAN VIOLETS. POSTER OF SOME SORT OF PRIEST ON THE WALL. I CALLED TOMMY.

...HE WAS ACTUALLY KIND OF SWEETLY WORRIED. MAYBE ERIC HAD LIT INTO HIM... OR MAYBE HE'D CALCULATED THAT HE COULD AFFORD TO BE CONCERNED BECAUSE, WITH THE NOR'EASTER WHIPPING NEW ENGLAND INTO A NASTY MERINGUE OF SNOW AND SLUSH AND ROAD SALT, HE KNEW THAT THE HIGHWAYS WERE CLOSED AND HE WAS OFF THE HOOK, AT THE MOMENT ANYWAY, SO FAR AS MY RESCUE WAS CONCERNED.

IT WAS CHANUKAH AND I WAS DETERMINED TO LIGHT THE CANDLES EACH NIGHT, EVEN THOUGH WE WERE ON THE ROAD. WE HAD A TINY TRAVEL MENORAH and CANDLES AND WE LIT THEM IN ALL SORTS OF UN- HEATED YOUTH HOSTELS AND PLACES LIKE THAT. ONE NIGHT WE WERE TAKING AN OVERNIGHT TRAIN FROM SOMEWHERE TO SOMEWHERE AND THE OTHER 2 GUYS IN OUR COMPARTMENT WERE CLEARLY OF ARABIC DESCENT.

I THOUGHT THAT MAYBE WE'D TAKE THE NIGHT OFF BUT TOMMY, IN A RARE SHOW OF CHARACTER, INSISTED. SO WE LIT THEM. AND OUR TRAVELING COMPANIONS WERE ACTUALLY NICE ABOUT IT. WE EXCHANGED FRUIT and TOBLERONE AS GIFTS...

TOBLERONE

DURING MY TRAIN STORY, EVE SPRANG OVER TO A PLASTIC ORGANIZER FULL OF KITCHENY STUFF AND PULLED OUT A ROLL OF FOIL...

...AND STARTED TO MOLD IT INTO SOMETHING...

WHICH BECAME THE UGLIEST, LOVELIEST MENORAH I'VE EVER SEEN.

Oak Street, 1981

MY FATHER WAS SO ATTACHED TO THE HOUSE THAT MY MOTHER BASICALLY SAID, "TAKE IT, SO LONG AS I CAN GET THE HELL OUT OF HERE." AND BY THE WAY, I'LL TAKE THE KIDS AND THE CAT.

And so we moved across town.

I was in the seventh grade, awkward, afraid, and manically sex-hungry in a way I've never been since. Puberty struck me with peculiar force. It was a strange time and there we were in a new, unfurnished house in the same town. We didn't escape very far. I went to the same school. I had the same lack of friends. But somehow a mere change of angle made everything very different. My loneliness was somehow more profound. I felt, oddly, newly made. Not better — I just wasn't exactly the me I was when we all lived in my father's house. The move — and my newly found vocation (even now when I think of the house on Oak Street I see myself in the closet, soccer cleats on, masturbating to Christie Brinkley) — made this the beginning of something.

This was December 1981. The new house smelled of plastic. It was quiet, mercifully quiet. My father's rages were across town, and we only heard an echo. To make our not-yet-furnished house homier, my mother, bless her, put up a Christmas tree. We were Christmas-tree Jews. Let me be clear: we had no relationship to Christ beyond loving the mall like everyone else in America. And let's be honest: presents are better when they come all at once in a blitzkrieg of wonderful commercialism. Still, my mother never left out Chanukah. In fact, for her this was the holiday, and in her way she kept it purer by giving us trinkets — bottle openers, whistles, finger puppets — rather than bicycles those eight days. I remember the three of us, my brother, mother, and I, sitting on the floor in the dark beside the unlit Christmas tree. We weren't poor, but the illusion that we might become so was thrilling. My mother put the menorah on a folding chair and lit the candles and sang the prayer. I think this is the point I want to make. My mother sang.

> Let me be clear: we had no relationship to Christ beyond loving the mall like everyone else in America.

She so rarely ever sang. Her prayer was low like a hum, and very beautiful, and my brother and I listened and watched her face in the candlelight. I realize now that she was so young then. That so much was ahead of her. But she was my mother. How was I to know?

If there is symbolism in our celebrating in an empty house after escaping from my father — let it be. Farewell, Antiochus, it's been good to know you. It was our time of happy exile. We'd moved down in the world. Bless downward mobility as you bless everything else. But think mostly of my mother's voice. The menorah on the chair. A house that smells of plastic. Her voice like a hum, rising, rising.

Dolls of the World

THE MOVE WAS SCHEDULED FOR LATE JUNE, BUT THE CALLS STARTED COMING IN APRIL. MY PARENTS HAD RETIRED. THEIR NEW HOME — THREE THOUSAND MILES AWAY; A CONDO IN A SAN JOSE RETIREMENT COMMUNITY — WAS A FRACTION OF THE SIZE OF THE HOUSE IN WHICH I'D MOSTLY GROWN UP. THERE WOULD NOT BE ROOM FOR, SAY, A COLLECTION OF EVENING GOWNS SPANNING THE FOUR DECADES OF my parents' marriage — from a New Look – style red satin to a sleek, dolman-sleeved shift, loaded with linebacker-sized shoulder pads — or an elaborate set of Waterford goblets, five-piece service for twelve, which would not have looked out of place on Edith Wharton's most formal table. In California, life would be casual. My mother would buy new clothes, new dishes, new furniture, all trimmed and modern. But before she did so, she needed to get rid of the old stuff, a lifetime's worth of anniversary presents and birthday presents and Mother's Day presents, of Nambe vases and silver-handled fruit knives and needlepoint renderings of "Oriental"-style flowers, of fondue pots, iced-tea spoons, and toothpick holders, of Braun electric hand mixers, banquet-sized coffee percolators, and automatic foot massagers.

All of these things — and, of course, many more — had for years been neatly stowed in kitchen cabinets, in the rows and rows of built-in closets my mother installed in our massive basement, in the squat Ethan Allen buffet in our dining room. After Passover, my mother began removing them. And the phone calls began: Did I want the Balinese bark prints we'd picked up at Cost Plus when I was four? What about Grandma Pearl's love seat? The gallon-sized turquoise thermos we occasionally took to the lake? Those fondue pots? Twenty-four miniature cocktail forks carved out of ivory? The etched-glass martini glasses my mother had registered for in 1951 but had never liked and had rarely used? The sheets I'd slept on as a young child, imprinted with a repeating image of Raggedy Ann and Andy at play? Or those I'd switched to at eight or nine, a

> **Did I want the Balinese bark prints we'd pick up at Cost Plus when I was four? What about Grandma Pearl's love seat?**

Laura Ashley print of pink, nearly abstract rosebuds? The lamp in the family room with the pear-shaped glass base?

"Sure," I said, nervously, wondering where I would put all this stuff, wondering if I really wanted it. I was twenty-five and made $265 per week as an assistant at a literary agency. Most of my belongings came from the enormous Salvation Army in Astoria. It would be foolish to refuse anything, and yet, as my mother named thing after thing, I felt increasingly inclined to say no. I could not, somehow, imagine a future in which I gave dinner parties elaborate and large enough to necessitate several identical sets of crystal and-silver salt and pepper shakers, after which my guests would lounge on my mother's cream-colored sofa, delicately sipping aperitifs from the smaller siblings of those maligned martini glasses. My mother sold the crystal, a souvenir from a trip to Ireland, for $15,000. I suggested that my sister might like the living room sofa.

The calls kept coming. At work, I swiveled on my chair and glanced at manuscripts as she listed the things she'd unearthed in the cedar closet. "Years ago, when B. Altman's went out of business, I bought two glass plates — one for Amy and one for you — and I *completely* forgot about them. Oh, Joanna, they're *gorgeous*. Yours has a print of irises."

"I've packed up your room," she told me in May.

"I was planning on coming home and doing that," I told her, in carefully measured tones.

"Well, I couldn't wait," she said. "Anyway. And I've packed up some other silver odds and ends for you. The little candy dish. The fish trivet. But what about the menorah?" I struggled to picture my parents' menorah. Was it brass? It hadn't figured prominently in my childhood mythology. Before I could answer, she said, "You have Grandma's, right?"

I had recently moved into my grandmother's apartment on the Lower East Side, which came equipped with a small, mildly confounding array of Judaica, including, actually, three different menorahs.

"I do," I told her.

"Okay, then I'm going to give ours to Amy. I think she lost hers in the move." This was a polite reference to both my sister's difficulty with maintaining ownership and upkeep of physical objects (including, but not limited to, her house, which had recently been covered in a volcanic spray of sewage, the result of neglecting their rural septic system for as many years as they'd lived in the place) and the fact that she'd recently left her husband and their three children — temporarily, we were told — and moved into a one-bedroom apartment in Poughkeepsie, somehow misplacing various family objects on the five-mile journey.

"Sure, that sounds good," I told her. "All I really want are the books. Whatever Amy wants is fine with me."

What Amy wanted, in the end, was most everything — or, at

least, all the big stuff — and this was, indeed, fine with me. Her house, as it happened, was not actually hers. My parents, I'd just discovered, owned it. And they'd decided to sell it, to cut my sister — eighteen years my elder — and her husband off.

"We're going to be on a fixed income," my father explained. "We can't keep up that house anymore. We can't support them. They can save up and buy their own place."

An entire house's worth of furniture wouldn't fit in my sister's little apartment, so my mother arranged for it to be transported to a storage facility nearby. And I, on a chilly night in early June, drove a dilapidated van out of the barbed-wire-rimmed U-Haul lot on the Bowery, picked up the man who would, a few months later, become my husband, and drove upstate. The next day, I began slicing open box after box — my second bedroom was a sea of brown cardboard — and unfolding protective sheets of bubble wrap and newspaper and tissue. A white Wedgwood vase. Two copies of *The Joys of Yiddish*. A pewter pitcher with a pattern of vines snaking up and down its face. One grandmother's flatware, then another's. (My sister, I was told, had received yet another set.) The steel canister set — stamped SUGAR, FLOUR, TEA, COFFEE in the sans serif font popular in midcentury — that had sat on our kitchen counter, supplying the ingredients for hundreds of cookies and cakes and brownies. Worn wooden spoons. The painted glass lamp that had sat by my bedside through childhood. The green enamel pots my mother had bought when she moved into our old house, twenty miles south, in Nyack, a town I much preferred to our own. Four yellow pillowcases, never used, in a Marimekko-ish butterfly print. (Where were the matching sheets? I wondered.) A sari-fabric dancing dress with a handkerchief hem. My beloved ice skates — Riedell silver stars — and my skis and ski poles and ski boots, the latter still in the original box, with its stark black-and-white design. Linen tablecloths and damask tablecloths and cotton tablecloths embroidered with flowers. The heavy glass candy dish that had sat on the coffee table in our living room, the sole spot of color in my mother's palette. My parents' vast and wildly colored collection of liquor, which dated back to the earlier years of their marriage, when they entertained avidly: Chartreuse and Cherry Heering and Sabra and blue curaçao and Harveys Bristol Cream and Vandermint and amaretto.

By the time I came along, these bottles had been banished to a dark recess of the stereo cabinet, which ran along one side of our living room. Come Thanksgiving — when the extended network of Rakoffs and Avruts and Merlises and Senators tended to gather at our house — my father might pry the door open and, under the wary eye of my mother, gather the ingredients to make martinis for the various cousins who liked to hit the sauce. But at Chanukah, the cabinet remained firmly shut. Barring the occasional invitation to eat latkes at, say, the Siegels', we spent the holiday alone, with minimal to no merrymaking.

Blue-and silver-wrapped presents were piled under and on top of the grand piano just north of the stereo cabinet; a blocky electric menorah was placed in the large front window. It was my job to twist the blue, ovoid bulbs into their sockets each night, as dark fell. Our real menorah — which was, yes, I was remembering, definitely brass — stayed in the kitchen, candles having been deemed too messy for the living room. Each night, before dinner and after lighting both menorahs, I sat in the dim, chilly room and quietly opened one gift, slitting the tape along the seams, just as my mother did.

Nearly twenty years later my habits hadn't much changed. As the day grew dark — and I grew sweatier, dustier, my hands darkened with newsprint — I found myself surrounded by a swarm of neatly opened boxes, their flaps yawning. There were things that were missing: the tall, delicate pot that completed my Aunt Fritzi's chocolate set (not that I had any use for a chocolate set; not that I was even sure what a chocolate set *was*); a Mexican blouse, embroidered all over with flowers; set of pastel portraits that had hung in our family room, that had probably — and deservedly — gone to my sister; and, most heartbreakingly, my dolls, which had sat, glassy-eyed and squat-legged, on the top tier of my white bookshelf for as long as I could remember. I'd expected to find them tucked into the corners of boxes, swaddled in stray pillowcases: the Russian peasant doll with real human hair; the china lady-doll with crumbling hoop skirt and parasol; the Japanese fabric doll, in elaborate kimono and obi; and, my favorite, the set of peachy-skinned, shiny-haired, plastic-bodied creatures known as "Dolls of the World," which had played key roles in my multipart Barbie dramas. But there were no dolls to be found, save a battered rubber Kewpie in a faded orange dress.

When I creakily rose from the floor — ready to shower; *not* ready to find a place for the thousand objects I'd just unpacked — I saw I'd left one box unopened, a box labeled LARGE SILVER. Once again, I pulled out the Swiss Army knife — itself a relic, survivor of umpteen summers at Camp Tel Yehudah, rescued from my dresser by my father — sliced open the packing tape, and began unwrapping soft, brown swathes of Pacific cloth. Serving pieces piled up around me, clattering on the worn parquet. There was the little candy dish — as a child, I'd filled it with halvah and jelly rings before company came — and the trivet shaped like a fish. The covered serving dishes, with their ornate curlicued handles, that had held boiled vegetables as recently as this past Passover. A set of small, tailored candlesticks. And then I found one last cloth bag, which contained something solid and heavy and large enough to fill the bottom of the box. "The menorah," I thought for some reason, before remembering that no, that had gone to my sister. With weary hands, I pried the thing out and unzipped the bag. Inside was a round platter, with a solid center and a thick filigreed edge, at the center of which was a lengthy inscription. It had, it seemed, been given to my mother by the Sisterhood of a synagogue called Sons of Israel to commemorate her five years of service as the president of said organization.

"Sons of Israel?" I thought. There were exactly three synagogues in the vicinity of the town in which I'd spent most of my childhood — the town we'd moved to when I was three; the town my parents would soon be leaving — and none of them were called Sons of Israel. "*President* of the *Sisterhood*?" The mother I knew had no interest in religion — less than no interest. Her most potent memory from early childhood had to do with the tyranny of Orthodoxy: one of her aunts accidentally mixed up the milk silver and the meat silver; their father, her Grandfather Abraham, became so enraged that he threw both sets through the kitchen window. ("*Through* the window," she liked to say. "Not *out* the window.") When my father fondly recalled his own father's small shul on Norfolk Street, my mother said, "Oh, come on. *Your father* took you out for shrimp chow mein on Saturdays." She was not, as far as I knew, a believer.

OUR TOWN WAS the sort of Jewish enclave that springs up, mysteriously, outside of New York — and, I suppose, D.C., Boston, and Chicago — but my friends were not Rachel Weissman and Jillian Altchek. They were Sudha David, Zinnia Yoon, and Susan Conachey. At their houses I ate samosas and kimchi and, most remarkably, that cliché of clichés: anemic sandwiches consisting of one slice of bologna, another of American cheese, and two of white bread. None of this struck me as odd—or struck me at all, actually—until my eighth year, when the majority of my classmates began attending Hebrew school. Tuesday and Thursday afternoons, as the rest of Mrs. Cohen's third-grade class piled into cars, en route to Pomona Jewish Center (Conservative) or Temple Beth El (Reform) or Monsey Jewish Center ("Conservadox"), I boarded a near-empty bus back to Tamarack Lane, where I sat at the kitchen table and ate Danish butter cookies with my mother. That I preferred this activity to any other—certainly to any involving the other attendees of Lime Kiln Elementary School—made me vaguely uncomfortable, but I squelched such concerns with military-style force and retired to the family room, where, beneath those aforementioned portraits of beautiful, big-eyed children—the sort popular in the 1970s—that sat atop the Danish modern bookshelf, my vast collection of Barbie dolls served as actors in an elaborate saga involving a costume ball, a grandmother trapped in an attic, and a private production of *As You Like It* (a play within a play!), the précis of which I'd recently read in Charles and Mary Lamb's *Tales from Shakespeare.*

But come December, it became clear that something was very wrong. My Jewish classmates were, this year, talking about Chanukah in a new, enticing way. They were going to parties at which doughnuts were served and dreidels were spun and songs were sung and gifts were picked blind out of big bins. And they were also — how had I never noticed this? — recounting their families' celebrations, which involved grandmothers and aunts and uncles coming in from out of town and making big batches of latkes, and which reminded me of passages from one of my favorite series of books, Sydney Taylor's All-of-a-Kind Family, a chronicle of a big Jewish family on the Lower East Side at the turn of the century. The sisters — Ella and Henny and Sarah and Charlotte and Gertie — bought pickles and penny candy and ate them on their stoop, when they weren't curling their hair with hot tongs or making costumes for Purim or helping their mother prepare for Shabbos dinner. Even while dusting, these girls had fun — true, boisterous *fun* of a sort I'd never quite experienced, living, essentially, like an only child in our pale, quiet house — and it occurred to me that they, like my classmates, went to Hebrew school.

Cautiously, I broached the subject with my mother. She explained that to attend Hebrew school one had to belong to a synagogue, and we did not belong to a synagogue because my parents — my mother — didn't like any of the options. Pomona Jewish Center, she felt, was "materialistic": their dues were unbelievably high, their members the sort of women who would soon come to be known as Jewish American Princesses (their children were my most popular, and poisonous, classmates).

Services at Temple Beth El were, she said, akin to "going to church." Monsey Jewish Center was located dangerously close to the Hasidic neighborhood of New Square. Of this, my mother could only shake her head in horror.

The real problem, of course, lay not in the synagogues, with their various flaws, but in my parents' faith, or lack thereof.

"We're not sure we believe in God," my mother finally explained.

"Things have happened," my father chimed in, turning his face toward his shoes, as he did whenever difficult subjects (like my sister) arose, "that made us think there might not be a God."

They were, I assumed, talking about the Holocaust. This made sense to me. I had read Anne Frank's *Diary of a Young Girl*—and was working my way through every other Holocaust- or World War II–themed novel I could find at the library—and while I didn't begrudge Anne's right to "believe, in spite of everything, that people are truly good at heart," it seemed to me, with my knowledge of her fate, that a God might have allowed some wandering in the desert, some enslavement, some slaying of sons, but He or She would not, could not have stood for the attempted extermination of his allegedly chosen people. "Oh," I told my father. "Okay."

> **The real problem, of course, lay not in the synagogues, with their various flaws, but in my parents' faith, or lack thereof.**

All of this went a ways toward explaining my family's interpretation of Chanukah, which struck me, by comparison, as rather like those bologna sandwiches Susan Conachey's mother served: thin, anemic. Not just because my parents didn't even feign an interest in Judah Maccabaeus, not just because no blessings were mumbled as we lit the candles, but because — and you have already guessed this, no doubt — they lacked the gaiety that I seemed, recently, to be hearing much about. Occasionally, latkes made an appearance on the holiday table, but only occasionally; my mother didn't love to cook, in general, and, in particular, disliked anything that "made a big mess." Standing over a frying pan for the better part of an evening, getting splattered with an ever-graying batch of batter and hot spurts of corn oil, was definitely not on her list of favored tasks. But what baffled me was that while our family was large and mostly clustered in and around New York and Palo Alto, we never gathered at Chanukah, the way, it seemed, other families did. Even my sister was generally off doing, as my mother said, "who knows what."

That year — my eighth year, the third grade — as the holiday was nearly upon us, my mother noticed that something was bothering me. I was quiet, reserved. She attributed this to feelings of alienation (though she didn't use that word) from the dominant culture of our nation. One night as I lay on my bed reading, she knocked on my door and came and sat down beside me. "It's hard to be Jewish at Christmas," she said, in the low pitch she used for serious talks. "Everyone is having fun. It's *seductive —*" This word embarrassed me, with its sexual connotations (I had read Beverly Cleary's *Fifteen* and the entire Judy Blume oeuvre). "It's *really* seductive. I know, trust me. The trees, the lights, the carols. It's beautiful. You want to be a part of it." I nodded and stuck my finger in my book. She must, I supposed, have been thinking of the tall fir in Susan Conachey's living room, or the Bing Crosby on the radio, which my father liked to sing along to, or the elaborate, buttery pastries we'd eaten a few nights back at the rustic home of some German immigrants, friends of friends.

But I, of course, didn't care about any of that. Christmas as practiced in contemporary America — the overly shiny ornaments, the illuminated Santas perched on rooftops, the synthetic red stockings with names inscribed in glitter — had little interest for me. The news reports of parents standing on line all night outside of Toys "R" Us to secure Atari consoles and Rubik's Cubes made me flush with shame. Worse still was the idea of compiling lists — of *asking* for what you wanted. But Christmas as it was lived in the books I read obsessively, over and over, filled me with a sick longing, rooted less in the specifics of religion, and more in the general ethos of the holiday, as embodied by various

> "It's hard to be Jewish at Christmas," she said. "It's *seductive.*"

nineteenth-century novels, first and foremost Louisa May Alcott's *Little Women*.

What I wanted was a Chanukah as redolent of — as informed by — ingrained, unself-conscious tradition as the March girls' Christmas. I could imagine nothing better than to be a March girl — preferably my namesake, Jo (and in an alternate universe, in which she, not Amy, marries Laurie) — eating roasted chestnuts and donating my dinner to the poor family down the road and trading scrappy, heartfelt gifts, each chosen *specifically* for the intended recipient, with careful thought given to what she wanted, what she loved, what she might, in her heart of hearts, truly *need*.

But what *was* an authentic Chanukah for an American family? The truth is, there was no such thing. We grown-ups are now all too coolly aware of Chanukah's minimal religious significance, that it was a minor holiday, artificially boosted to Christmas-level status in the 1920s by a double-team effort on the part of Jewish leaders — who had watched the latest wave of Jewish immigrants rushing to partake of Christmas ("The purchase of Christmas gifts is one of the first things that proves one is no longer a greenhorn," a reporter asserted in the *Forward* in 1904) — and canny marketers, who began advertising their wares as ideal Chanukah gifts (and, in the case of Aunt Jemima flour, ingredients) in the then-booming Jewish press. Tellingly, the All-of-a-Kind Family books are filled with vivid descriptions of Purim and Passover and Sukkot but scarcely touch on Chanukah. My parents, born in the 1920s, had barely celebrated the holiday. My classmates, well, their parents were closer in age to my sister — they were baby boomers — and they were, in a way, the first generation to take for granted the import of the holiday as a consumer occasion and, to be fair, one for gathering family, Noel style, or, in my dream life, March-family style.

But I was not Jo March and, perhaps more important, my sister was no Meg March (though it occurs to me now that she bore certain similarities to *her* March namesake, the artistic, bratty Amy). For starters, she barely knew me. She'd left for art school soon after my birth but had quickly dropped out to marry, then divorce, a blond, mustached man with the improbable name of John Johnson and a charming tax-free business involving the sale of mood-altering chemicals. At my parents' behest — and with their financial backing, of course — she went to nursing school somewhere in the vicinity of our house, but she was rarely around. Throughout my childhood she would occasionally appear on our doorstep, her hair a different length or color — now choppy and short, one strand dyed blue; now tawny and long and permed — jumping furiously into my parents' arms, pouring herself one of my dad's Cokes, hunching tensely in an armchair while my father sat at the secretary in the living room and scrawled out a check for her, then racing off again in whatever little car she was driving at the time. I was always relieved to see her go, and ashamed of my relief.

Occasionally, her visits coincided with major holidays — and one year, my birthday — and this year, this eighth year, she would, it seemed, be around for Chanukah, or one night of it. In the spring, she would be getting married again (though we all pretended that her first marriage had never happened), this time to someone deemed acceptable by my parents: an X-ray technician and would-be doctor, Jewish, from Bricktown, New Jersey. His name was David and he liked to cook. This year, there would be latkes.

As Chanukah came closer, the gifts began to appear under the piano. Eight boxes of identical shape and size, with my name on each of them. This was unprecedented, and I was curious. On the first night, we lit the candles — my mother allowing me to hold the *shamash* by myself, for the first time — and the electric menorah; then my mother said, "Are you ready to open a present?"

Strangely, I felt nervous. What could be inside those identical boxes? "Um, okay," I said.

She looked them over carefully, squinting at some incomprehensible marking in the corners, then handed me one. "I think this one should be first."

Carefully, I peeled off the wrapping paper and found a thin cardboard box with a clear plastic window at the front. DOLLS

OF THE WORLD it said, in black letters, above the window. POLAND it said below. Behind the window stood a small doll with honey-colored braids, a dirndl skirt, and a funny peaked cloth hat.

"Wow," I said. "Cool."

My mother beamed. "I saw them and I just couldn't resist," she said. "I would have loved these when I was your age. Amy had something like them, but they've disappeared, I think." Removed from the box, the Polish-costumed doll blinked at me. "I thought you should open Poland first," my mother explained, "because — well, you know — your Grandma Pearl's family was from Warsaw." I nodded but felt deeply confused. My grandmother and her sisters all had deep-black eyes and blue-black hair.

One by one, the dolls emerged: Spain, dark-haired, in a red-and-white polka-dot flamenco dress. Greece, with a black velvet vest and a wildly striped skirt. Italy, in a thin red, white, and green ensemble that seemed more a nod to the country's flag than its indigenous costumes. Being the diligent, dorky child I was, I brought each new doll into the family room and compared her dress to the portraits of native peoples in my *Encyclopaedia Britannica* set. To my surprise, they appeared to be fairly accurate.

On the eighth night, my sister and David arrived, full of chatter about the wedding and my sister's new job, in a psych unit at

Cornell Medical Center. I showed her my dolls, the last of which I'd just opened: Sweden. I was still dismayed by their physical characteristics: Why was it that the Spanish doll was the one that most resembled me, when our family had come from Russia and Poland?

"Well, Polish people — actual Polish people — are generally fair," my mother said. "And Jews can be from Poland, but they're still Jews. They don't look like Poles, usually. So maybe if there were an Israeli doll it would look like you. Or an American doll."

I nodded. "Or a Jewish doll," I said confidently and was surprised when my mother laughed. "I don't think they would make a *Jewish* doll," she said. "It would be an Israeli doll."

My sister folded the dolls' legs and sat them in a row on the floor of the family room, as if they were watching television.

"I can't remember if I still played with dolls when I was your age," she said. "I was never that into them. I always wanted to play outside." I nodded solemnly. My mother had said the same thing. Amy had scars all over her legs from falling off roofs and out of trees, while I had to literally be pushed out my front door when the warm weather hit. "But dolls are cool," she said. "I love these dresses. They're really pretty."

I thought about asking her why there couldn't be a Jewish doll but instead found myself pointing to the pastel portraits on top of the bookcase.

"Who are they?" I asked. It had not occurred to me, until the words left my mouth, that they *were* anyone — anyone other than anonymous, beautiful faces, like the faces of princes and princesses in fairy tales. And as soon as I finished the sentence, I saw that this was the wrong question to ask — and also the right one. My sister's face had gone blank and slack.

"You know who they are," she said.

"No," I said. "I don't."

"You do," she insisted. I shook my head. Sighing, she pointed to the girl on the right, with dark hair and green eyes under thick brows. "That's me," she said.

"You!" I almost shouted.

"Yes," she said, and drew her lips in a thin line. "And that's Anita" — she pointed to the blond girl, my favorite of the three, with her shy, wide smile and kind eyes — "and that's Mark. My brother and — *our* brother and sister."

I wasn't sure what to say, what else to ask. Suddenly, many things made sense. The questioning of God. The sudden sadness that came over my parents, like a summer storm. "There was an accident," she said. "I was there, too —" And then she turned away. "Mom and Dad can tell you," she said. "They'll tell you when you're old enough." I nodded. "I'm going to find David," she said. "Okay?" Okay, I said. Okay.

But it was never okay. They never told me. There was an accident, I knew, and my brother and sister had died. My sister, a cousin eventually revealed, had been in a coma for weeks or months — the cousin couldn't remember; "It was a horrible time," he said — and awoke changed. "She had brain damage?" I asked. "No," my cousin said. "She couldn't live with the guilt. She was the one driving the car."

IN CALIFORNIA, MY parents thrived. Our rapidly multiplying Palo Alto relatives — the cousins with whom my mother had been raised, like siblings, and their children and grandchildren — gathered weekly for potluck dinners and held big, unruly Seders. "You would love it here," they told me. "So would Evan." At our wedding, in October, they gave us a large, shiny brass menorah in a traditional style of interlocking arches. It was a grand-looking thing, and Evan — who preferred silver to brass, matte to shiny, modern to traditional — looked at it doubtfully, then tucked it in the linen closet, behind the million sheets and tablecloths I'd unpacked three months prior, and next to the monstrous silver platter, the origins of which I'd still not figured out. But in December, I pulled the menorah out and placed it on top of our piano, a mahogany baby grand with a cracked soundboard, inherited, along with the apartment, from my grandmother. Each night we lit the candles — I had learned the blessing as a teenager, at camp — and the glow, brighter each night, reflected back the warm sheen of the Wurlitzer, casting long shadows on our pristine walls. By the last night, Evan was won over. The menorah stayed on the piano through the new year, then moved to the old yellow bookcase in the foyer, the first thing visitors see when they enter our apartment—the first thing we see when we come home.

Exactly a year after their move, my parents returned to New York for a visit. For a few days they stayed with Evan and me on the Lower East Side—the vases and fruit knives and fondue pots they'd bequeathed us now neatly stashed in our crumbling kitchen—before heading upstate to visit with my sister, who had returned to her family. My sister and her husband had not, of course, been able to buy a new house—or even an apartment—and after a brief, disastrous stay in a friend's cottage (they'd flooded the place; the friend was suing), they'd moved into a residence motel, of sorts, with a two-story medieval knight in its parking lot. My parents were not pleased. "Amy's a blonde," my mother sighed, wearily, into the phone at the Poughkeepsie Holiday Inn (they'd dismissed the knight-guarded motel as "sleazy"; a fair assessment, I would soon discover). "Not just a blonde, a *platinum* blonde."

That weekend, my husband and I drove up the Taconic and checked into the Holiday Inn. Moments later, my mother burst

> The menorah moved to the old yellow bookcase in the foyer, the first thing visitors see when they enter our apartment—the first thing we see when we come home.

into our room, suggested that Evan play a round of golf with my father, and hustled me off on some invented errand. As soon as we hit Route 9, she said, "It's all gone. Everything is gone."

I didn't understand. "What's gone?"

"Everything," she said. "Everything. She didn't make the payments on the storage facility. Not even one. They sent her three warnings, then they auctioned everything off."

"You're kidding," I said, for this seemed a real possibility to me, more possible, somehow, than my sister's losing everything, the material sum of my parents' life together. (Later, when I told a close friend what had happened, she was shockingly nonplussed. "Amy fucked up again," she said. "Big surprise.")

"I should have given you Grandma Pearl's love seat," my mother said.

"And the menorah," I said. She gave me a funny look.

"What menorah?"

"*Our* menorah," I said, with a hint of impatience.

"I didn't give Amy our menorah," she said. "What would Daddy and I use? *We* still need to light the candles, don't we?" I assented that they did. "I love that menorah," she said, with a smile. "We've used it for years. And you know what's funny? I can't even remember where it came from." This was indeed funny, coming from a woman who could recall the provenance of every dress she'd ever placed on her back. "Why would we give Amy our menorah?" she asked again.

"You said—" I began, then stopped. What was the point? Then, suddenly, I remembered the portraits—the pastel portraits of Amy, Anita, and Mark. Had she given them to Amy? I felt slightly panicky at the thought of this. "Hey," I said. "What's Sons of Israel?" I asked instead, surprising myself.

"Sons of *Israel*?" she said, all trace of laughter gone. "It's the synagogue in Nyack. Why?"

"Nyack, our Nyack? Where we lived when I was a baby?" She nodded. "There's a platter. It was in one of the boxes you gave me. From the sisterhood—" Suddenly, I felt uncomfortable. This was not, I was sure, something she would want to talk about. Not now, certainly, but maybe not ever. And I had known this; this was why I'd waited so long to ask.

She nodded again and swallowed. "We were founding members," she said. "Back before you were born. Way back. Mark had his bar mitzvah there. Before the accident—" I nodded quickly to cut her off. If you had asked me, at the time, I would have said I wanted to spare her the pain of talking about my brother and sister. But now I suppose it was a selfish move: I was terrified of what she might say. She went on anyway. "Afterward, we just couldn't go back. With everyone feeling sorry for us. We were always reminded of them. Everywhere we looked. We had to move away."

For a moment, we sat, and then she unbuckled her seat belt and, with a grin, pointed to the T. J. Maxx. "Should we go shopping? It seems like we deserve some new stuff."

"Sure," I said.

As we walked across the cracked pavement, along the rows and rows of nearly identical cars, she put her arm around me and I remembered:

"My dolls," I said. "Amy had my dolls."

"No, she didn't," my mother said quietly.

"She *did*," I said, hating the slight whine that crept into my voice. I was supposed to be the strong child, the mature child, the wise child. I was the child of their old age, the child who would take care of everything, who would right all my sister's wrongs and replicate every joy of those I was conceived to replace. I was the child who never asked for anything. But I wanted my dolls. "You accidentally gave them to her. Just like the butterfly sheets."

"No, I *didn't*," she insisted, her voice rising, and I knew, for sure, that she was going to cry. We were approaching the sidewalk, the threshold of the store, where rack after rack of clothing awaited her gimlet eye, her expert knowledge of cut and drape and fabric and make. "I would *never* give Amy your dolls. How could you say that? You loved those dolls. They were your *friends*."

"But I didn't find — "

"I packed them away in a box, a ski box, a square box with a handle — "

"A *ski* box?" I asked.

"A ski *boot* box," she said. "A Salomon box. Wasn't there a Salomon box?"

There was, I told her, and guided her inside.

That night, we made an attempt to eat dinner together as a family at a steak house favored by my youngest nephew, then six. But my mother was furious and couldn't even look in the direction of my sister, who was indeed as blond as Madonna, with bangs like Sandra Dee's. After the waitress took our order, Amy began sobbing. My teenaged niece looked like she wanted to hide under the table. My brother-in-law pretended everything was fine. Eventually, Amy left the table and never came back. We spent the rest of the night searching for her. The next day, Evan and I drove home in silence, through a hot, heavy rain. In the front closet, on the highest shelf, next to my ice skates and Evan's basketball, I found the black-and-white box — I'd saved it, as a teen, because I'd liked the design — brought it into our bedroom, and opened it up. The dolls were packed in layers, like candy. I pulled out the Japanese lady, the china lady with her parasol, a black-haired flapper doll, the Russian doll, her wiry hair disintegrating. And there, below them, were the Dolls of the World, their bright costumes a tangle of rickrack and ribbons and wide-brimmed hats and black Mary Janes, their blue eyes still blinking, their cheeks still dewy and fresh, their hair still shiny and thick. One by one, I pulled them out — their plasticky scent still strong, still familiar after all these years — and read off the names of their countries, imprinted in gold on the bottoms of their shoes. Spain, Mexico, Holland, Poland, Greece, Italy, France, Sweden.

"Hello," I said to them. "Hello," I said.

"You're still here," I said. "You're home."

Chanukah Glutton

THE CANDLES ARE LIT, THE SONGS SUNG, AND THE FRENZY IS UNDER WAY. "PRESENTS!" MY SONS SHRIEK. THEY'VE BEEN PLANNING WHAT THEY WANT SINCE LAST CHANUKAH, SCRUTINIZING CATALOGS, INFORMING RELATIVES, BEGGING, PLOTTING, PLEADING. BY THE TIME THE HOLIDAY HAS ACTUALLY ARRIVED, THEIR GLEE HAS REACHED TOWERING PROPORTIONS. I HAVEN'T EVEN SET THE GIFT-WRAPPED PACKAGES ON the floor when they grab and tear into them with a rapacity I had forgotten they possessed. Seconds later, our living room is an orgiastic banquet of Lego and Fisher-Price, the wrapping paper and ribbons scattered like carcasses around the room.

As responsible, presumably conscientious parents, we, of course don't buy presents for every night. But in addition to the one or two we buy, there are gifts from grandparents and aunts and uncles, many of whom are at our house for this first of many nights of celebration. As best I can, I ration the presents, stagger big ones and little ones, give books even though, to my writerly embarrassment and chagrin, my older son is of the belief that books do not count as presents. I manage to hide a few gifts for a later date, to be pulled out in moments of parental desperation. I wish we had done what a circulating e-mail suggested: designate one night for big gifts, one for small, one for homemade, one for charity. We've tried to emphasize the other parts of the holiday. We've donated to local toy drives. My kids know the story of the miracle. They know the blessings and the songs, from the Debbie Friedman Chanukah CD that has played, for the past month, in a continuous loop in our car. But even so, ask my kids what their favorite holiday is, and they will scream "Chanukah!" Ask them why and they will scream the answer with glee.

> **To my writerly embarrassment and chagrin, my older son is of the belief that books do not count as presents.**

As the kids construct a miniature city on our living room floor — the Playmobil police station next to the Lego firehouse and playhouse, transportation between them provided courtesy of the Fisher-Price school bus and the giant Tonka dump truck—I go into the kitchen, ready to fire up the frying pan. In this holiday devoid of much ritual, the process of calling my grandmother for her recipe (which I then lose from year to year), and then hand-grating the potatoes and onions makes me feel like it's Chanukah. But even though it's her recipe, I've never been able to master the delicate lacy latkes my grandmother produces. Mine are thick and hefty, leaving an oil slick on the paper towels where they drain.

I'm determined to eat only one. The week before Chanukah may not be the best time to join Weight Watchers, but a post-baby five pounds has bothered me for the three ensuing years since my second son was born, so long that it's getting harder to truthfully blame them on a pregnancy. Filled with optimism and resolve, and the impending holiday notwithstanding, I decided to join, bringing home from an introductory meeting and weigh-in my point-counting kit, my booklet to look up each food I ate, and a calendar in which to record every bite.

But faced with latkes, my willpower lasts briefly, and soon I've got my own feeding frenzy going on in the kitchen. I'm just tasting them, I tell myself, to make sure I've seasoned them enough. Then I'm just having my one latke now, before dinner. Then I'm just eating two, still a reasonable number. As I keep surreptitiously eating latkes, my sister, who is visiting from New York, wanders in to keep me company. We stand over the frying pan, talking and picking at the latkes. She's done well with her gift choices for the kids: Blues Clues Boogie Woogie Juke Box and Lego Blizzard Blaster have risen to the top of the pile and are being played with to great delight. Despite my misgivings, it is a nice sound to hear, their exuberant thrill, their reveling in the gifts.

> **The week before Chanukah may not be the best time to join Weight Watchers.**
>
> ∽☙∽

In our family, gift giving tapers off by the time you reach adulthood, but my sister and I reminisce about our childhood Chanukahs. Of course, there are other things we remember besides the presents. We remember rifling through the box of candles and choosing the ones for our menorahs, either arranging multicolored patterns or opting for the seemingly righteous alternation of blue and white. And my mother playing "Maoz Tzur" on the piano, as we, in our none-too-melodious voices, sang along. But overshadowing these memories is the image of myself as a toy-crazed kid.

First there was Baby Alive, who peed, pooped, and vomited after being bottle-fed different powdered formulas. I would die, I thought, if I didn't get Baby Alive. I cried until I got it, and undeterred by the inevitable disappointment when those bodily functions didn't work as advertised, I cried for the Snow White china doll, then for the corresponding seven dwarfs. To my further writerly embarrassment, I remember my horror, one night, one year, when my mother dared give me a book for a present. Most of all, I remember the anticipatory delight when my parents went out a week or so before the holiday on a mysterious errand, and then later, knowing that the presents were hidden somewhere in the house. They were *in the house!* Not able to settle for waiting, my siblings and I would search the premises. We always found them, because though my mother went to the effort of hiding them, she usually chose the same spot, the cabinet above the washing machine, onto which we would climb to catch these sacrosanct glimpses of what was to come.

"I've got to stop eating these," I finally say to my sister. By this point, I feel stuffed. My face feels coated in oil, as if I've not only ingested it but bathed in it. Why did I eat all these? I berate myself. In the face of such excess, the pleasure quickly fades. I've spent my Weight Watchers points not just for the day but for the week. The only way to recoup this expenditure will be to fast for the duration of the holiday.

"Do you think I could bake the rest of these?" I wonder, only halfway done with my potato mixture and already having used a whole bottle of oil, more than I usually use in a few months of cooking.

But there's no such thing as baked latkes. Well, technically there probably is. If there exists salmon gefilte fish, tricolored matzo balls, white-bean-and-lamb cholent, surely somewhere out there, in a gourmet low-fat kosher cookbook, is a recipe for baked latkes. But Chanukah commemorates not the miracle of the potato but the miracle of oil. Without an abundance of oil, doesn't a potato pancake cease to be a latke, or at least to be one that is relevant to Chanukah?

It's not only the miracle of oil that commemorates a little becoming a lot. The other, less mentioned part of the holiday is the military victory where the few Maccabees defeated the many Greeks. As long as I'm counting, it's not just the oil and the Maccabees that were scarce in number. In the Talmud, there are only seven pages that discuss Chanukah, a scant number compared to Purim, another nonbiblical holiday, which has both the Book of Esther and an entire tractate in the Talmud detailing its laws. And not to spoil the fun, but the current celebration of Chanukah itself is a case of something small becoming large, a decidedly minor Jewish holiday coming to occupy a prominent space in American Jewish life.

In those few Talmudic pages is the (relatively, I suppose) famous debate between the two rival sages Hillel and Shammai as to whether to ascend or descend in the number of candles lit each night. On most topics, Jewish law is decided according to Hillel, and in this case it is too. Shammai, who bears — perhaps unjustly — a reputation as a more curmudgeonly scholar, thought that we should begin with eight candles and reduce the number each night. The more magnanimous Hillel believed in starting with one candle and adding to that each subsequent night.

It was this debate that we learned about in Jewish day school, when it was time to turn to Chanukah. We took sides in the debate, acted it out, searched for the symbolic meanings in the two opinions. Do we look at what has passed or what is to come? Do we increase our celebration each night or decrease it? we asked, in a Talmudic version of the question about the glass being half empty or half full. But still, you couldn't fill a few weeks of class time with this. So while for Passover we filled notebooks with laws, bringing home photocopied sheets with various diagrams of the required amount of

> **Chanukah was a minor blip on the calendar, a way station between Sukkot and Pesach.**
>
> ∽❦∽

matzo to be consumed at the Seder, Chanukah was a minor blip on the calendar, a waystation between Sukkot and Pesach. These eight days didn't hold a candle to the life-halting fall holidays or to the domestic upheaval that is Passover cleaning, where running a toothpick along the grooves of a dining room chair in search of crumbs is considered normal, even required.

One can only imagine what Hillel and Shammai might say about all this gift giving: Do we add or take away, diminish the festivities or increase them? But as a relatively recent phenomenon, presents aren't mentioned in a classic rabbinic discussions. (Traditionally, Chanukah gelt was given, which evolved into the giving of chocolate coins, though I am loath to imagine what would happen if I handed my kids either a quarter or a yellow mesh bag of chocolate coins and said, That's it for tonight.) Dreidels and latkes make few appearances too. But what is discussed, and indeed required by the rabbis, is the obligation to give thanks. That, in fact, is one of the central themes of the holiday, one that is generally forgotten once the festivities are under way.

Rather than make the obligatory Christmas reference, I prefer to invoke the American celebration of Thanksgiving. There too is an abundance, with its banquetlike table crowned by a turkey and all its fixings. But even after I emerge from that table, having gorged on stuffing (it's not only latkes that are my weakness), the holiday doesn't have a particularly gluttonous feel to it. And I think it's because the abundance is tempered by gratitude, and by the realization that it didn't have to turn out this way.

Just as one vial of oil didn't have to become eight. Too little didn't have to become enough. And, in fact, it didn't, for so many generations, and still doesn't for so many people. The extra oil, the twenty-thousand-piece Lego set, even dearly departed Baby Alive should feel like a celebration of abundance. So long as the gratitude part isn't just the quick thank-you at the end of the evening but a central, defining tenet of the holiday. The menorah burns brighter when you know that you really had only enough oil for one day, when the remaining seven days of light truly feel like a gift.

Which is not to excuse commercialism or materialism, not even to justify overeating; it is hard to recognize gifts when we are so accustomed to getting them. And in what at least in my experience is the dizzyingly busy and ego-damaging endeavor called parenting, it's hard to impart this message or any message. And so, above the din of the present assembling and the searching for AA batteries to power all these new electronic toys, I hear another sage opinion. It's the voice of the Weight Watchers leader, around whom I had felt sheepish in the first place. Having heard stories of people trying to lose thirty, fifty, seventy-five pounds, these five pounds hardly seemed reason enough to be there. "Portion control," she said, and to underscore the point, she wrote it, in all caps, on the dry-erase board. It's not that some foods are bad while others are good, she then expounded. You have to know what your body needs. Learn to recognize when you feel satisfied.

Where does that point of satisfaction lie? Somewhere between rigid limits and orgiastic frenzies, somewhere between one latke and the to-remain-untold number that I consumed. Next year, I promise myself, we will actually implement some greater present-control plan. For at least one of the nights. Or maybe for two. And when my kids do bask in the muchness that is before them, I want them to at least see it not as their due but as an abundance, for which we should be immensely grateful. Maybe next year, even if I'm no longer counting Weight Watcher points, I will find a recipe for baked latkes. Or at least oven-fry them. Meanwhile, a few days into the holiday, the frenzy has begun to subside. At least until their birthdays, my kids are spent, sated, stuffed. As for me, I'm sick of latkes. Improbably, I think of a song from an upcoming holiday, which my kids will relearn when we switch the CD from Debbie Friedman's Chanukah to Paul Zim's Passover songs. *Dayenu.* It's enough.

> **Where does that point of satisfaction lie? Somewhere between rigid limits and orgiastic frenzies, somewhere between one latke and the to-remain-untold number that I consumed.**

My Peaceful and Glorious Brothers

I DIDN'T ALWAYS THINK OF CHANUKAH AND VIO-LENCE SIDE BY SIDE. I'M SURE THERE WERE PLENTY OF PEACEFUL CHANUKAH NIGHTS DURING MY CHILD-HOOD, BUT MOST OF THEM PROBABLY OCCURRED BE-FORE MY MEMORY KICKED IN AND MY BROTHERS WERE BORN. THERE ARE THREE OF US AND I'M THE OLDEST, WHICH MEANS I HAD ALL THE ATTENTION TO MYSELF for close to two years. Then Arthur arrived on the scene. Four years after that, Jeffrey came along. Three boys, eight nights, approximately twenty-four presents. Do the math. It added up to trouble.

No disrespect to Jeffrey, and thank God he found his way here, and I would never, ever wish for fewer brothers. Still, sometimes I wonder if it would have been easier for my parents with just two of us. As my friends with kids like to tell me, two versus three is the difference between man-to-man defense and zone defense. It's tough to stop the run or block the shot when you're outnumbered. My girlfriend, however, doesn't follow sports.

> Three boys, eight nights, approximately twenty-four presents. Do the math. It added up to trouble.

When I attempt to explain, she tries to persuade me to move beyond such a competitive metaphor. She talks about yoga. She claims it's not about offense or defense, winning or losing. Like everyone in the ashram or whatever you call it isn't hoping to breathe better than the person one mat over. Get that third eye open before anyone else. Anyhow, she believes that the spacing between siblings is more important than the number of siblings. In other words, she wants a big family. A Chanukah with thirty-two or forty presents, I guess. I'll need to get a raise. I'll need to get a second job. So will she.

But, for the moment, I'm discussing the past, back when my thoughts were simply about being a kid, not about having one or seven. Before Jeffrey appeared, Arthur and I shared a room, and we seemed to get along fine. We had to turn the lights off and climb into bed by a certain hour, but as long as we kept quiet we could stay up as late as we wanted. Sometimes, we'd smell popcorn being made in the kitchen, and that usually meant we were allowed to sneak downstairs and have some. More often, though, we'd keep ourselves awake by trading the various toys we stored on the shelves by our beds. The terms of those late-night trades were vague. We softly tossed what we had — Hot Wheels, Super Balls, yo-yos — back and forth. The goal was to send the objects safely and silently from mattress to mattress. To the uninitiated, it might have looked as if we were throwing things at each other. But we were sharing.

Really.

After Jeffrey was born, my parents hired contractors to add a few rooms to the house so that everyone could have their own space. I got my parents' old room, Arthur got the room we used to share, Jeffrey got what had once been the den, and my parents got a new bedroom with a private bath, as well as a new den with plenty of room for my father's small gun collection, which he kept under lock and key. We should have all been happy, right? Well, it was complicated. Mom was disappointed because after three tries, she still didn't have a daughter (though she never would have wished for fewer sons — or at least not that often and rarely out loud). Dad wasn't thrilled because he had to cook dinner more often since Mom needed to go back to work because business was bad and the construction of the new rooms had been expensive. It didn't help that she wound up working the graveyard shift as a registered nurse. She was awake when we were asleep, sleeping when we were awake. Attention was harder to come by, and Arthur, Jeffrey, and I competed for it. Dad kept telling us to behave ourselves. He cooked a lot of macaroni and cheese with chopped-up hot dogs mixed in. Fortunately, he knew how to make a mean black-and-white milkshake. And when he heated up an apple pie, he cut it into quarters, a wise way not only to avoid leftovers but also to defuse yet another fight over who got the bigger piece.

And so our five-person family went from day to day, moving as best we could between moments of relative calm and moments of minor crisis.

Then Chanukah would roll around.

There were, weeks in advance, elaborate preparations behind closed doors. That was part of the problem. No doubt Dad had good intentions. Looking back now as a guy seriously contemplating the possibility of kids, I think I can understand some of what was going on behind those doors. First of all, my father has always been highly organized. A former paratrooper in the Air Force Reserves and an ex-scoutmaster, he believes deeply in being prepared and in packing your own bags with extreme care. (That parachute needs to open!) He tends to pack his bags several weeks before traveling out of town (he's a salesman, like his father before him). Sometimes, when he can't find a particular article of clothing, he realizes it's in a suitcase that's ready for an upcoming (i.e., a week or two away) trip. Second, my father was an only child of older parents, an experience that left him longing for siblings and for a more caring mom and dad. Combine the commitment to preparation with the desire for a larger, loving family and, apparently, you get a Chanukah full of jealousy, recrimination, and time-outs.

But before all of that, before the holiday began, there were exquisitely wrapped presents arranged on the buffet in the dining room. Each of us had our own clearly labeled stack. We were allowed to pick up our gifts and shake them, and in those moments of pure possibility — the boxes might contain anything! — we could do our best to guess the contents of each box. However, we did this guesswork at our own risk. If we broke the gift, it was our own tough luck. And there was no guarantee that we were evaluating useful information, since my father enjoyed stuffing the boxes with extraneous and noisy items — marbles, paper clips, pencils. He knew how to make a sweater sound like it might be a Pachinko game. And vice versa.

Of course, we should have been grateful for whatever we were given. Our parents hadn't had much luxury in their lives, they hadn't had the opportunity to go to college, and their short vacations consisted of little more than a crowded car ride from the Philadelphia suburbs to the Jersey Shore and back again. Year after year, they worked hard to provide better lives for the three of us. We should have unwrapped their presents and rejoiced. On every one of those eight nights we should have sprinted across the room to hug our ridiculously unselfish parents. I mean, why

> **Night after night, we chose to break as many commandments as possible.**
>
> ❧

not? Wouldn't that have been easier and more relaxing than all the fighting and shouting? We could have adjourned to the basement playroom to test out the toys together. On the nights we found clothes or books in our boxes, we shouldn't have complained that those were the worst gifts, exactly what we didn't want more of. We should have tried on the shirts, taken turns reading aloud to each other.

But, instead, night after night, we chose to break as many commandments as possible: we dishonored our mother and father, coveted the presents we weren't given, took various names in vain, including the Lord's, treated certain toys like gods, thought murderous thoughts, lied, stole, and so on. It was as if, for us, the eight nights of Chanukah created the need for eight Days of Atonement (at least!).

GIVEN THOSE ANNUAL struggles, it makes sense to me that the festival of lights comes from a story steeped in violence. But I didn't know how much violence was involved in the story of the Maccabees until my father gave me a copy of Howard

Fast's *My Glorious Brothers* as one of my Chanukah gifts. I don't remember which year he gave it to me—I might have been eleven or twelve. Whenever it was, I'm sure I was disappointed. I probably said something charming, like "Great, another book. Just what I need." Still, I read it. I read almost everything he gave me.

At Hebrew school, I'd heard about the oil that miraculously burned for eight days in the reconsecrated Temple, but it wasn't until I read Fast's novel that I learned how long and how viciously the Maccabees had fought with swords and hammers and their bare hands to reach the point where they could even worry about the oil and the Temple. *My Glorious Brothers* is full of bloody wars waged around Jerusalem, full of sacrifice and vengeance and death, full of descriptions like this: "With his bare hands, Judas killed [Apelles], lifting him by the neck and snapping it suddenly, as you do with a chicken, so that the wild squeals stopped and the head lolled"; "We rolled on the ground, he trying to draw his sword, I cursing the neck plates that impeded my fingers. He half drew his sword, and I stopped trying to throttle him, but beat his face in with my clenched fist and continued to beat at the bloody face even after he was dead." In perhaps the most brutal and memorable of the many battles, the Maccabees come face-to-face with a mercenary army equipped with tanklike elephants:

Eleazar leaped ahead and alone he met one elephant that had out-paced the others. Such a sight was never seen before then or since, for Eleazar's great body arched, the hammer swung back over his head, and then it met the elephant with a crushing thud that sounded above the screaming and shouting. And the elephant, skull crushed, went down on its knees, rolled over and died. . . . Eleazar fought with his hammer until a blow from an elephant's tusk tore it from his grasp. It was not as long as it takes here in the telling. He was dead before Judas and I could reach his side.

Howard Fast was, in many ways, a heroic figure, a prolific, hardworking, and fascinating writer who fought against HUAC and the blacklist, a man more than worthy of his own essay, but I wasn't aware of that when I read *My Glorious Brothers* as a kid. I raced through those pages the same way I raced through the stories of outer space and spies and the Wild West my father had given me over the years.

Yes, I was the kind of kid who carried a paperback book everywhere I went and, like my father, I concealed each book in a special vinyl book cover so that no one could see the title. If someone asked me, "What are you reading?" I answered the same way my father answered me: "A book." If they stubbornly tried again, asking, "What's it about?" I had my follow-up response ready. I'd flip to the end and say, "It's about three hundred and thirty pages."

I was, as I said, charming. The sort of kid, really, who de-
served no Chanukah gifts at all. Not only did I fight with my
brothers, but I was also obnoxious to relatives and strangers. At
the same time, however, I remained my father's son. I carefully
packed my bag for school every night before I went to sleep. And
I read those paperbacks.

All that reading was surely an attempt to grow closer to my
father, but it wasn't a closeness that led to in-depth discussions
of what we'd read. He read to escape, not to analyze. If I asked
my father what he liked about a particular book, he tended to
say either that the writer was able to "paint with words" or that
the story kept him "turning the pages." Then he'd tell me that
if I liked that one, he had another for me. There was, it seemed,
an endless supply.

But *My Glorious Brothers* was an exception because it led to
a longer conversation. When I finished that novel, my father invited me into the new den, closed the door, and told me to sit
down. "I'm tired of the three of you always fighting," he said.
"You're brothers. You know I wish I'd had some brothers when
I was growing up. Your mother says that someday you'll realize
how lucky you are to have each other. Well, I'd like that someday
to be now."

I'd heard versions of this before — I was the oldest, so I was
supposed to set an example; I was supposed to be my brothers'
keeper; I was supposed to be the man of the house when Dad was

away, though I found that this didn't carry much weight with my mother. In any case, I said what I usually said: "I'll try."

"I want you to try harder this time," my father said. "I hope you learned from this book that if you and your brothers ever truly have to fight, you should learn to fight together, like the Maccabees did."

I couldn't imagine ever fighting like the Maccabees did. I probably couldn't even lift one of their swords, let alone brain an elephant with an enormous hammer. The truth was, I had no desire to fight against my brothers. It wasn't something I planned. In the abstract, when I was alone, I loved Arthur and Jeffrey completely. But when we were together, something else took over. I *could* try harder and, once again, I promised myself that I would. "Sure," I said. "Okay."

At that point, I figured the conversation was over. Dad would hand me another book and I'd be on my way. Not this time, it turned out.

"I want to show you a few things," my father said. "I think you're ready."

In the past, when my father talked about his time in the Air Force, he was self-deprecating and vague. His love for planes had always been clear — he'd often stop in the middle of a conversation to gaze up into the sky at a passing jet, as if he expected to see one of his fellow ex-paratroopers dropping down to visit — but all he'd say about those years in the Reserves was that people called him Jew-boy. He also joked that he was much taller before the 250 jumps from twelve thousand feet compacted him.

Now, in the den, with the door closed, Dad started talking about how he'd studied hand-to-hand combat. He told me there was no such thing as a fair fight. He told me you could kill someone if you hit them hard enough in the right way on the bridge of their nose. He told me the throat was a good place to punch a person. He unlocked the cabinet where he kept his guns, but instead of pulling out a gun, he handed me another book, a small manual filled with illustrated instructions about what to do if someone attacked you with a knife, if someone was choking you, if someone attacked you with two knives.

I tried to pay attention as my father explained a few basic moves — always step away from a punch, always keep your guard up and your head down. I tried to picture myself clobbering some of my school's bullies, but I couldn't get that image to come into focus. Who was I kidding? I was a scrawny boy who read paperback books. Then my father reached into the cabinet again and pulled out a rifle.

His gun collection was no secret, another relic of his Air Force years, but this was the first time he'd actually taken one of the guns out of the locked cabinet and shown it to me. Becoming the man of house was suddenly something very scary and serious. My father told me it might one day be up to me to save the

> My father told me it might one day be up to me to save the family. He showed me how to load a clip and how to push a clip into the gun.
>
> ∽⊘∾

family. He showed me where he kept the key to the cabinet and where he stored the boxes of ammunition. He showed me how to load a clip and how to push a clip into the gun. "If someone ever breaks into the house while you're here," he said, "let them take whatever they want. The telephone is your first and best weapon. But you should know about these weapons, too."

I didn't want to touch the gun. I had no desire to hold it in my hands. I wanted to see my father lock it back up in the cabinet.

"Look," he said. "Watch what I'm doing."

Once again, I tried to pay attention. Unfortunately, I needed to use the bathroom.

Some Maccabee I'd make.

I SUPPOSE THAT conversation could have been the beginning of a different kind of father-son relationship, an initiation into one sort of adult male world. I could have developed a love of firearms and fighter planes and martial arts. On more than one occasion, my father had mentioned to me his dream that I would not only go to college but would win a scholarship to Annapolis or the Air Force Academy. There in the den, I could have moved closer to becoming that son.

Many things began to change, but I didn't veer toward the military. (Decades later, however, I was offered a job as an English professor at Annapolis; I took a job elsewhere.) Still, I wanted to keep reading those adventure stories, and maybe even write a few. I just didn't want to live them. My father, to his credit, recognized that. After our Howard Fast conversation, the guns never came out of the cabinet again. Together, my parents pushed me to choose the college that felt right to me, and they paid the bills that made it possible for me to enjoy what they'd never had.

They did the same for Arthur and Jeffrey. I became a writer and professor, Arthur became a marine biologist, and Jeffrey became a lawyer. Honorable but soft professions all, or so it sometimes seems to me. We certainly wouldn't fare well against a robber or a bully or an elephant-riding mercenary. We wouldn't fare well against much that this harsh world has to offer so many of its inhabitants.

I can't say that I read *My Glorious Brothers*, glimpsed my father's rifle, and then immediately renounced violence, never to fight with Arthur and Jeffrey again. It wasn't quite that simple. But the three of us did gradually learn to treasure the fact that we get to live in this world together. Though we stopped celebrating Chanukah long ago, we have learned to appreciate the incredible gift our parents gave us by giving us one another. Someday, hopefully, we'll begin to repay that gift by giving our parents some grandkids.

(My poor mother! Three sons and still no grandchildren! But that's a subject for another essay.)

Maybe, in the end, in my family, Chanukah is a kids' holiday, and maybe this isn't necessarily a terrible thing. It's a holiday rooted in violence that ultimately teaches children to appreciate the blessing of being free from violence — if we're fortunate enough, if we can somehow, in today's world, ever actually be free from violence.

Still, I do wish there were a different story behind and in front of it all. I'd love for us to find a way past the ongoing, all-too-predictable narrative of precious oil, ruined temples, and deadly battles. Sometime before I have kids, I'd like for there to be a more peaceful Chanukah tradition. But I've read enough to know it's not really possible to change the past. These days, I'm hoping that my lovely, flexible, noncompetitive, big-family-dreaming girlfriend will help me work on changing the story of the future.

Oh, Lord. Oh, Lourdes. Alors!

I GREW UP IN BANGOR, MAINE, IN AN ANTHILL JEWISH COMMUNITY DOMINATED BY CATHOLICS AND PROTESTANTS. MY BEST FRIEND WAS POLLYANNE MEAD, WHOSE FATHER WAS A POLICEMAN. FROM THE WALLS OF EVERY ROOM IN HER HOUSE HUNG TECHNICOLOR PHOTOGRAPHS OF JESUS, HIS HALO CASTING a mournful, otherworldly light over features more beautiful than those of any movie star at the Bijou Theater's Saturday matinee. Pollyanne's brother Frankie used to torment us as we played with our dolls under a Jesus portrait and next to one or another of the statues of the Virgin Mary that dotted the tables, even the dinette set. "Sissies," he'd taunt. Then he'd turn to me. "Christ killer," he'd add.

"Don't mind him," Pollyanne would say. "He's got no manners." Did manners mask the truth? I wondered. And did Pollyanne agree with such slander but choose to remain tactful? I wanted to ask, but I kept my mouth shut.

If I'd killed Christ, it was something we never discussed at home. Though politics got analyzed and argued over at every meal, religion seemed to be as off-limits as sex. My mother's grandfather had been the first rabbi in Bangor; his son, my grandfather, was an atheist. My mother aspired to WASPdom; she worshipped Boston Brahmins the way Pollyanne's family worshipped Jesus. Her favorite novel was *The Late George Apley*, her favorite family, the Adams. She was suspicious of anything that reeked of "nouveau." She liked old furniture and faded carpets and falling-apart cars. Our old falling-apart house was nothing like the spiffy subdivisions in the development called "Little Israel," where a lot of the Jewish community lived. How bad for your character were dishwashers and thick wall-to-wall and power steering and showers, I considered, turning the separate spigots that alternately froze or scalded you.

> **If I'd killed Christ, it was something we never discussed at home.**
>
> ༄

My mother didn't belong to the Jewish organizations that the mothers of my Jewish friends had joined — Hadassah, the Sisterhood, the JCC. She was the proud integrator — Bangor's James

Meredith or Charlayne Hunter-Gault—of formerly restrictive groups, the only Jewish woman on the board of the Y, the Family Service Committee, the only Jewish member of the Athena Club. She was notorious—and proud of the fact—for arriving at bar mitzvah celebrations after the service and just when the reception would start. She poured cocktails at five o'clock and preferred watercress sandwiches with the

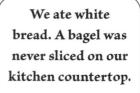

We ate white bread. A bagel was never sliced on our kitchen countertop.

crusts cut off to chopped liver on rye. We ate white bread. A bagel was never sliced on our kitchen countertop. Thus, it was hardly surprising that Chanukah did not brighten any of our cold, dark December dusks. Unlike the Jewish families who stressed the eight days of Chanukah as payback for Christmas, our mother knew there was no comparison. She gave us Christmas.

Of a sort. If we owned no menorah or even one of those white plastic ersatz pines advertised at W. T. Grant's as a "Chanukah bush," we also boasted—in some perverse, equal-opportunity holiday sense of fairness—no tree, no Christmas lights or decorations, no Bing Crosby "White Christmas" on the hi-fi, no jolly Santa figures about to burst into "Ho ho ho." But if we didn't have the Santa figures, we had Santa. We left peanut butter and jelly sandwiches out for him along with a brimming glass of milk, placed near the draftiest window to keep it cold. On Christmas Eve, my mother stomped on the roof with her heaviest boots and scraped something—a shovel?—along the shingles to approximate the sound of a sleigh. And though I worried about how Santa would visit my sister and me in a household without a fireplace, every Christmas morning brought presents tied with ribbons. The sandwiches had disappeared, a few crumbs dotting the plate. The glass was empty, except for a ring of milk encircling the rim. In their place was an envelope—return address: the North Pole—which enclosed a proper thank-you note. According to our mother, no situation existed that didn't warrant a lesson in etiquette.

Though my father participated in this *let's not disappoint the children* activity to a certain degree, he led a secret life that both mystified and excluded me. Mornings, I saw him wrap strange things around his arm, attach a little leather box to his forehead, sling a striped and fringed shawl over his shoulders, and rock back and forth. "What's he doing?" I'd ask my mother.

"Prayers," she'd dismiss.

My father had grown up in a kosher house. My father prayed. My father went to the synagogue. These were things better ignored—a secret family shame, like drinking or adultery.

Meanwhile, my friends and cousins used to head to the synagogue for potato pancake parties, latke bake-offs. I heard the stories. How Norman Kaminsky scraped his skin right into the potatoes. How the blood from the boys' knuckles seasoned the pancakes. I made excuses for being left out of this raucous merriment, these peculiar rituals. Would I ever want to taste Norman Kaminsky's blood? Would I ever want to eat the skin from my classmates' knuckles? Besides, I also heard all about the unfair division of labor: the boys won the honor of grating the potatoes; the girls had simply to fry them.

"Why can't we get a menorah?" I'd ask my mother.

"And leave those candles burning?" She'd cringe. She who set ablaze dozens of white tapers in their antique candlesticks on the sideboard and dining table for Saturday night dinner parties. "Besides," she replied, "you have Hebrew school and Aunt Edie and Uncle Abe and Uncle Arthur."

Yes, I went to Hebrew school. Why, I couldn't understand. Perhaps it was a cheap means of babysitting while my mother attended board meetings and bridge games; and later, when my father got sick and could hardly make it out of bed to his law office, a way to keep me out of the house. I had Chanukah at Hebrew school. I twirled a dreidel and ate some of those boy-grated, girl-fried potato pancakes, now cold and stale. That should have been more than enough, implied my mother. Especially if you take into account Aunt Edie, Uncle Abe, and Uncle Arthur, my father's maiden sister and bachelor brothers, who filled in all the many holes, festival-wise, for my sister and me and my first cousins. My uncles and aunt shared a house on Palm Street that was a refuge for us nieces and nephews when life become unsatisfactory under our own roofs. There were seven of us, the oldest child in each family — Marilyn, Marshall, Mameve, Mark — named for my father's mother, the sainted Mamie, who died before we were born and whose sons — six of them — so adored her, the legend goes, that they would carry her on their backs when she was too old and weak to walk. Her photographs were no less enshrined in the rooms of her six sons and one daughter than Pollyanne Mead's various Jesuses and Madonnas. And no less worshipped either, I was sure.

With the exception of Passover — which Uncle Sam and Aunt Lil (Marilyn's parents) held, as they possessed the biggest table — Abe, Arthur, and Edie's kitchen was control central for all Jewish high and low holiday celebrations. (We, of course, by unanimous vote, hosted ecumenical, New England Thanksgiving.) On Palm Street we could light the menorah. We could collect eight days of gold-wrapped chocolate Chanukah gelt. And the real thing, too — crisp dollar bills, which might, depending on report cards and Hebrew school attendance and dreidel skill, increase exponentially, so that on the eighth day there'd be quite the tidy sum to buy the tap shoes or the American Flyer we were coveting. Uncle Arthur had 78s of Jewish music, which only years later did I come to identify as klezmer. Every bowl and platter offered up potato pancakes and chicken soup and chopped liver and these sticky honey balls, the peasanty, ethnic food my mother would recoil from, food the Adams family and the late George Apley, and the ladies of the Athena Club and the likes of Pollyanne Mead would have trouble even pretending to taste, no matter the requirements of etiquette. Nothing felt so delicious and forbidden.

But then I lived a bifurcated life. Who was I? Was I my mother? Was I my father? Did I celebrate Chanukah or Christmas? Did I prefer Santa and Jesus and Mary or the Bible stories of Moses and Rachel and Sarah that we were reading in Hebrew school?

My confusion was not helped by my attendance at Mass for almost one solid year. On his way to work, my father would drop me off early at the Abraham Lincoln School, where my first-grade teacher, Miss O'Connor, would drag me along to seven o'clock Mass. It never occurred to me to tell my parents about these visits; such starts to my day seemed as ordinary as breakfast or brushing my teeth. At St. John's Church, I liked the Jesuses and the Madonnas better than the scarier ones in Pollyanne Mead's house. I liked the cushioned benches, the hushed voices, the kneeling pews, the clink of the rosary beads, the comforting murmur of prayers, less strange and startling than my father's silent bowing and the funny-looking things lashed around his arms and forehead. Was the blood of Jesus, the wine in the fancy goblet, more acceptable than the blood and scraped flesh of some boy's knuckles in the potato pancakes? At least, it appeared more dignified, somehow.

My first-grade Catholic year ended abruptly when, walking past St. John's with my father, I crossed myself.

Other things ended, too. My father stopped his prayers; he stopped ordering only halibut at restaurants, although we never kept kosher at home. He stopped going to the synagogue. He didn't walk with me, and when he did, he staggered. "Your father's a drunk," said Frankie Mead, the same kid who told me I killed Christ. But my father never drank. It was my mother who made those cocktails in the silver shaker, who poured cheap Don Popov vodka into antique decanters of crazed and bubbled glass, who opened bottles of maraschino cherries and olives stuffed with pimientos.

The summer after that year, my father went away to Boston, to what the grown-ups called, in hushed voices, "the sanatorium." When he came back, things changed. He rarely went to the office. He lay in bed or on the sofa. At night he moaned. Doctors made house calls. He yelled. He demanded. He criticized us. In the middle of most family dinners, though my mother was determined to carry on — candles lit, yards of silverware on either side of service plates — we left the table in tears. *Your father was so brilliant,* people said, talking about him in the third person, past tense. *He went to Harvard Law School from Bangor; he wrote those books on Maine law,* they marveled. I began to see him, in Catholic terms, as the cross we had to bear. There was no God or Jesus or Moses, no Santa or rabbi, no prayers in Hebrew or in Latin that could make him well.

It took him ten years to die. A disease of the central nervous

system. A virus, they thought. Maybe something to do with po-
lio, they said.

I joined the Jewish sorority and also the fancy high school
social club that inducted few Jews. So insecure about my own
social position, I never thought to refuse when they didn't invite any of my Jewish classmates. I had friends in Little Israel
and friends in the big Victorian mansions on Broadway. My best
friend was the daughter of the minister at All Souls' Congre-
gational Church. After delicate inquiries about dietary restric-
tions, her family invited me for parsimonious dinners of tuna
stuffed into tomatoes (one tomato apiece) and a small scoop of
vanilla ice cream for dessert. I ate lavishly at Aunt Edie, Uncle Abe, and Uncle Arthur's. I lit Chanukah candles on their
menorah and continued to accept the gold-wrapped chocolate
coins well after the age for such childish treats had passed. All
through college and into my twenties and thirties, envelopes
would come at Chanukah time — *a little Chanukah gelt,* they'd
say. *Love from Abe, Arthur, and Edith.* And out tumbled a much
welcomed check for eighteen dollars, the number that, in Hebrew letters, signifies long life.

While the freshly bar mitzvahed or newly graduated received
trips to Israel, I wanted nothing more than to go to Paris. I was
in love with all things French. Mostly, I was in love with my
French teacher, an Albanian named Efthim Economu, a teacher
of such extraordinary humor and charisma and enthusiasm he

seemed lit from within. *On your first trip to Paris,* he used to tell us, *you'll turn a corner on the Champs-Élysées, and there I'll be.*

Certain I'd found my own late George Apley as well as the focus for my private prayers, I memorized the Marseillaise. Lips pursed, I perfected the French *u*.

My freshman year of college, I traveled to Paris with my grandmother; the following summer, with my husband to be. At every corner I searched in vain for Monsieur Economu.

I married. My husband, who had grown up in a rigid Jewish house, celebrating Chanukah and every holiday joylessly, was relieved to leave difficult family associations behind.

Once we had our own children, everything changed again. We bought a menorah — a wild-looking, rough-hewn concoction on display at one of the Radcliffe pottery sales. We lit orange candles, which melted down the sides of the mottled clay and were nearly impossible to scrape off. We sought out dreidels in all sizes and colors. We gave the children eight days' worth of gold-covered coins. We chose Christmas presents, but nixed any kind of tree. We celebrated Thanksgiving, Passover, Chanukah, Kwanzaa, the High Holidays; we bought them chocolate Easter eggs. They voted against Hebrew school and bar mitzvahs, and we agreed, since their only regret seemed to be the gifts they'd miss. Both boys, in turn, visited Paris and Jerusalem.

Years later, when my first book came out, I went back to Bangor for a reading. There in the front row sat Monsieur Economu.

Was he eighty? Even older? I couldn't tell. He looked exactly the same to me. He laughed. His eyes twinkled. Charm poured off him with the pervasive intensity of his European-smelling cologne. He kissed me on both cheeks.

"I've been to Paris many times," I confessed, "and on each trip, I looked for you around every corner." I paused. "But you weren't there," I accused.

"Oh, yes I was," he said. "Alors! You just weren't looking hard enough."

That Christmas, I received a present from my editor, a young Irish-American whose parents still spoke with a brogue, a man much amused by my tales of my first-grade Catholic year. He had sent me a clear plastic Madonna filled with "genuine water from Lourdes." For months I had been complaining that my manuscript-in-progress required divine intervention, needed a cure. I velcroed the Madonna to my computer. Two days later, an envelope arrived in the mail, postmarked Bangor. I opened it. Inside was a card. A menorah graced the cover. Silver Hebrew letters embossed the top. Stars of David marched up the sides. Eight orange candles flamed. *Happy Chanukah,* the card read. Signed underneath were these words: *I hope you have a great holiday. Shalom. With love from your French teacher, Efthim Economu.*

We celebrated Thanksgiving, Passover, Chanukah, Kwanzaa, the High Holidays.

My Father's Menorah

MY FATHER HAD ALWAYS BEEN THE ARTIST IN OUR FAMILY, SO IT WAS NO SURPRISE WHO I SOUGHT OUT FOR HELP SHORTLY AFTER RABBI NATHAN ANNOUNCED THAT OUR HEBREW SCHOOL CLASS WOULD BE HOLDING A COMPETITION TO SEE WHICH ONE OF US COULD BUILD THE BEST MENORAH.

Though my father made his living as a radiologist, art was his avocation. He didn't tell me many stories of his past, but the most inspiring ones he offered were replete with tales of his own creativity. On Thirty-ninth and Drexel Avenue, on the South Side of Chicago, at S & L Beverages — his father's ill-fated soda pop factory that went out of business not long after the beginning of World War II when sugar became scarce — my dad helped to manage the factory's accounts and spent his spare time proposing new label designs. When S & L was sued by the Pepsi-Cola Company for producing a soft drink called Pep Cola, my dad proposed changing the product name to Loyal Clown Cola, a beverage that, in his vision, would have been advertised by a cartoon clown bearing a bouquet of balloons. My grandfather didn't take his son up on this proposal. While my father was still in high school, he worked part-time for the old *Chicago American* newspaper, designing layouts for Montgomery Ward advertisements. And on weekends, he took classes at the Art Institute of Chicago.

The house on Mozart Street, on the northwest side of the city in West Rogers Park, where my parents moved shortly after the births of their first two children, was, and still is, more than forty years later, a treasure trove of my father's artistic projects — some completed, some abandoned. Most blend whimsy with practicality and demonstrate my dad's talent for finding alternative uses for common objects. In a side room in our basement, a model train set is supported by barium barrels discarded from my father's radiology practice. The cardboard barrels, often beautified with collages made from covers of my father's favorite magazine, the British humor biweekly *Punch*, serve multiple functions in the Langer basement: storage, ornamentation, furniture. In one of those barrels is the preliminary model of a fountain that my mother always wanted my dad to build for our backyard garden.

Old pairs of pantyhose also found alternative uses in our basement. Placed on the end of a stick, they could be used as nets for trapping insects for school science projects; attached to the hose running out of the back of the washing machine, they directed soapy runoff water into the industrial sink.

In the basement room known to us as "the Pool Room," because of the regulation-size Brunswick pool table in it, all the furniture was designed by my father: pale orange, plastic chairs separated from each other by oblong tables with holes specially designed to hold ashtrays and drink cups; globe-shaped light fixtures operated by the slight turn of a golden key; a bar, which also occasionally functioned as a projection table for slide shows and eight millimeter films that my father shot. These films were viewed on a screen that could be pulled down to conceal a compact Zenith stereo system and a collection of records — my father liked listening to bagpipe music, Peggy Lee, and, occasionally, wolf calls from an album produced by *Natural History* magazine; he once played that record at top volume with the windows open in order to scare our Orthodox Jewish neighbors into thinking that a wolf pack had moved in on Mozart Street.

Elsewhere in the house on Mozart Street are other examples of my father's artistry: a sketch he drew of my sister at age twelve seated at his desk, completing her homework; the view of Michigan Avenue from one of his office windows; sketchbooks filled with charcoal and pencil drawings, predominately cityscapes.

Although my father's artistic tastes tended to be rather traditional, he did have a surrealist's penchant for framing artifacts that wouldn't typically be found in frames — an uncut sheet of dollar bills from the U.S. Treasury, a sheet of postage stamps commemorating the American bicentennial.

Few of the actual artworks on the walls of our house, save for a Ben Shahn poster in our living room, represented the work of any well-known artists. There was a painting of a school bus filled with children completed by my sister in grade school; also, photographs my brother or I had taken on various trips. Most of the original paintings were the work of Louis Katnic, one of my father's X-ray technicians, who had been wounded during World War I, and whose depictions of race cars, Mount Fuji, and one sad clown seated beside a sad, white poodle adorned our walls, not necessarily for their artistic merit but for the artist's loyalty and friendship to my father.

I don't remember much of my sister's bat mitzvah — held in my parents' basement when I was about three years old — save for some stray details, such as the fact that one of my sister's friends gave her a Blood, Sweat & Tears album featuring the song "Spinning Wheel"; also, my father went to his barber on that day and returned with an even shorter than usual crew cut, sporting an earring, and saying that he would attend the event dressed as Mr. Clean; and, most of all, the paintings my father created for our basement laundry room, which was where a good deal of the bat mitzvah action would take place.

Framing a mural depicting an idyllic picnic scene — complete with a red-and-white-checked tablecloth, bumblebees with rolling eyes, and a bisected bottle of Coca-Cola, a Miller High Life can, and a coffee cup to give the mural a three-dimensional aspect — were two thick, floor-to-ceiling heating pipes that my father had adorned with paintings of cheerful animals: a monkey, an owl, a yellow fish with green scales. Whenever I think about the day that will come at some point — when my mother moves out or sells the house on Mozart — this is what I sometimes feel I will miss most: not the front stoop, where I played Pinners or Ball-Against-the-Wall after school; not my bedroom, with its aqua-colored walls; not even my mom's pristine garden or her porch or my sister's canopy or my brother's chess set or my books or my manual Royal typewriter, but these simple, joyful paintings. And I wonder if there would be a way to write into any sales contract that, no matter who takes control of the premises, these must be preserved.

And then there were the artistic projects that involved the whole family; in these, my father truly excelled. The silent Super 8 films that my father shot may lack professional performances

> **My father went to his barber and returned with an even shorter than usual crew cut, sporting an earring, and saying that he would attend the bat mitzvah dressed as Mr. Clean.**

or a concise narrative flow, but these liabilities are more than compensated for by top-notch set and costume design: my headdress-clad brother playing an Indian brave banging on an elaborately painted cardboard drum; my first forays into motion-picture acting in literary adaptations — wearing a papier-mâché tiger mask and emerging from a garbage drum while playing the title role in *The Tiger and the Teapot;* picking construction-paper blueberries off a tree painted on a basement wall while playing *The Blueberry Pie Elf.*

I needed my father's help more than anyone with these and other family art projects, for I was, without a doubt, the worst artist in my family.

I do not say this to be self-effacing; I am merely stating fact. From an early age, I could write a decent story or take a fairly well-composed photograph. I was hardly a star musician, but I could muddle along with my piano, violin, or clarinet. When it came to art, however, I was an unmitigated disaster. My sister inherited my father's skill for artistry and design. My mother could always draw a reasonable boat. My brother perfected a signature cartoon character — a smiley-faced, bow-tied gent with a squiggle of hair emerging from the top of his head. But I'd live in eternal terror of seemingly endless Sunday drives in which my father would take all of us to the sloped lawn near the Adler Planetarium to sketch the Chicago skyline.

The concept of perspective completely eluded me. I couldn't

draw buildings, and when I tried to draw people, I always stumbled when it came to arms, legs, or necks. For a month, the students in Mrs. Lerman's art class painted a mural on the subject of war, and since I could not draw a tank or a gun or a soldier, I was given the only responsibility of which anyone thought me capable: drawing flags. I must have drawn hundreds — French flags, Japanese, and Italian, though not the American flag, for the proper distribution of stars and stripes was far too complicated for me. Recently, I came across an old report card; my art teacher wrote, "Adam tries very hard, but it is difficult for him to succeed in this area."

What little success I enjoyed in art was greatly abetted by my father, who, during my early grade school years, tried to inculcate in me the dual pleasures of art and medicine. He would encourage me to read a chapter about Anton van Leeuwenhoek in Paul de Kruif's *Microbe Hunters,* and he would try to teach me to draw Chicago White Sox pitcher Bart Johnson (a figure considerably more intriguing to me than Leeuwenhoek) by viewing Johnson's photo in the *Chicago Daily News* sports section not as one image, but as many separate squares that could be copied individually. He took me to his medical office at 720 North Michigan Avenue and taught me how to recognize tuberculosis and diverticulitis. And he helped me take my useless, *Sesame Street*–inspired bottle-cap collection and turn it into something more practical; with his close instruction, I made a map of South America by pressing

> **I made a map of South America by pressing the bottle caps into the top of a Styrofoam container that had once held a dozen Pfaelzer's steaks.**
>
> ∽◌∾

the bottle caps into the top of a Styrofoam container that had once held a dozen Pfaelzer's steaks.

My father helped me make a golden giraffe out of papier-mâché, helped me script Super 8 films for a JCC filmmaking class based on shorts he'd seen produced by the National Film Board of Canada, taught me how to use his prize Exakta camera, with its special film-editing blade, and made me my very own Chicago Blackhawks jersey, with an Indian Head painted on the front and my name stenciled on the back.

During grade school and my first two years at Hebrew school, my father was Cyrano de Bergerac to my Christian de Neuvillette — hiding behind the eaves and allowing me to take credit for an artistry that was not my own. For school Halloween pageants at Daniel Boone Elementary, I had no passion for the store-bought masks of my classmates, no interest in their hackneyed ghost and warlock costumes. I wanted my costumes patterned after disguises worn by Charlie Chaplin in his early, two-reel films, which my mom and I would take out of the library and watch at home in our basement. And so my father used construction paper and paint to dress me as a totem pole and a tree, thus allowing me to take home prizes in two separate pageants.

I had an idea for a board game that I would create for a project assigned in Mrs. Kantz's reading class. The game was based on Monopoly but set in Chicago, with miniature cars used as game pieces. My father drew the game on posterboard and made the automobiles out of construction paper, thus allowing me to become one of the only students to receive a passing grade on the assignment.

I even nabbed a Certificate of Merit and Honorable Mention from Lincoln Federal Savings and the Chicago Board of Education for a poster promoting thrift, which compensated for my lousy penmanship by using cut-up words from the covers of my dad's *Americana* magazines.

"I bet your mom helped you do that," a third-grader named Jim Kotowski told me. I could respond with absolute honesty, "No, my mom didn't help me at all."

A MENORAH DOES NOT require a particularly complicated design, but the only one I knew was the one that we kept in our dining room cabinet — a dull, tarnished model about nine inches high with eight arms of equal height and a Star of David behind the *shamash* holder. The candleholders were stained black with years of accumulated burnt wicks and wax drippings. So when Rabbi Nathan made the announcement regarding the menorah competition, I was stumped — I couldn't conceive of a menorah made out of anything but metal. Maybe I could work with paper or cardboard or wood, I thought, then figured that they would all burn, and I certainly didn't have any idea how to bend or shape metal.

K.I.N.S. Hebrew School of West Rogers Park was not a lavishly funded institution. The classrooms were small and cramped, desks were lopsided more often than not, and the only field trips I remember taking were to a yeshiva in Skokie and a matzo factory on Touhy Avenue. Thusly, the prizes that were being offered for the menorah competition were predictably frugal — a gift certificate for a free pizza at the Tel Aviv Kosher Pizzeria, a record of Jewish folk songs recorded by Theodore Bikel, a plastic chess-and-checkers set. But more important than any of these prizes to me was the fact that the three top vote getters would be displayed in our classroom window for all passersby on California Avenue to see. Which was reason enough for me to attempt to coax my father into helping me with my menorah design.

Although I was not yet eleven years old at the time of the competition, the period of my artistic collaboration with my father had already entered its decline. Perhaps he sensed that I was getting old enough to complete projects on my own. Or maybe he had simply grown weary of my artistic incompetence and realized that I would never become quite the son he had envisioned — it is true that, around this time, although my brother had already entered medical school, my father stopped taking me to his office and instead began recommending that I eventually pursue a career in law, a profession for which he had little respect. Or possibly my father had problems of his own that he chose not to divulge and did not want to be bothered with my silly menorah competition. I honestly cannot say.

If I were writing a novel or a short story, I would invent some crisis or turning point here — a family argument, a profound revelation, an unmendable rift between my parents. And I would present the menorah competition as one boy's desperate effort to bring his family closer together. But the sad truth is that I don't know why my Halloween costumes stopped being fanciful creations inspired by Chaplin films; nor do I know why my father stopped shooting Super 8 films or painting the walls of our basement. And as for the menorah competition, all I remember is the fact that I wanted to win and see my eight candles lighting the way up California Avenue, and my father, though he had demurred every time I had asked him up until the night before the competition deadline, ultimately agreed.

Within a half hour of that grudgingly spoken agreement, my father created something so easy and perfect that I couldn't help but feel somewhat ashamed that I had been unable to think of it myself. The design was classic Seymour Langer — a mixture of the whimsical and the pragmatic that created new uses for

> **The only field trips I remember taking were to a yeshiva in Skokie and a matzo factory on Touhy Avenue.**

found objects. From the kitchen junk drawer, where my dad kept his rubber bands, his rulers, his flashlight, and his matchbooks, he found a rectangular slab of wood and a sheet of golden tinfoil. He wrapped the slab in a section of the foil, then asked me to go to the porch, where we stored all of our board games, to find a box of old blocks. Once I had found the blocks, he selected nine wooden cylinders of differing heights. He drilled a hole in each, then wrapped them in the gold foil and glued them to the slab. Presto! A golden menorah.

The next afternoon, I brought my menorah to Rabbi Nathan's Hebrew school classroom, where a few of my classmates were already displaying theirs on the windowsill that gave onto California Avenue. I sized up the competition and declared myself an early favorite. The other constructions were either too un-original — menorahs made out of store-bought products such as Lincoln Logs or Tinkertoys — or too elaborate to be the work of a Hebrew school student — for instance, Yakov Golnick's twisting bouquet of soldered metal that was clearly the brainchild of his father, an engineer. What I particularly liked about my father's design was that it was creative enough to win admiration, but simple enough that an inspired student in Rabbi Nathan's *gimel* class conceivably could have devised it without any adult assistance.

After evening prayers, we carefully surveyed the menorahs with all the solemnity for a trivial cause that a group of 1950s homemakers might have brought to a blueberry-muffin-baking contest. We then ranked our top three choices on secret ballots. I was careful to put myself in first place, with my friends Avram Levine and Chaya Persky following behind, and to leave Yakov — whose father's labor seemed to be getting the most attention — off the ballot entirely.

The first sign of trouble came on the way out to recess, where we were to play Nerf football while Rabbi Nathan tallied up the ballots. Behind me, I heard one of my philistine fellow students say, in a voice that was probably not as hushed as she assumed it to be, "But it's just some wood wrapped in tinfoil." Titters ensued.

By the time we had returned from recess, I had resigned myself to a second-place finish, understanding that, to a class of ten- and eleven-year-olds, Yakov's flashy presentation would most probably beat out my father's subtle wit. But when Rabbi Nathan announced the winners, I had trouble concealing my disbelief or sense of outrage. Yes, Yakov Golnick would be enjoying a free pizza at the Tel Aviv, but my father's menorah didn't even finish in the top three. Again, if I were writing a novel, I would invent some meaningful reason why my menorah didn't win — maybe my father had written a secret message on the base of the menorah, such as "Adam needs to grow up and shouldn't rely on his father to do his work anymore, so don't vote for the schmuck." But nothing like that happened. I just didn't win. My classmates thought that, at minimum, three menorahs were better than my dad's.

Rabbi Nathan encouraged all of us whose menorahs wouldn't be displayed in the windows of our classroom to bring them home and enjoy them with our families, but I didn't bring mine home; I left it there on the windowsill, and at home on Chanukah, our family lit the candles using the same silver menorah as always. When I returned to Hebrew school after our winter holidays, only three menorahs remained in the classroom. Doubtless, mine was already in the trash.

Looking back on the anger and frustration I felt upon losing out in the menorah competition, I see not only the poor sportsmanship and sense of entitlement of someone who thought he needed to win at everything, but also the sadness of a boy who was seeing the slow disappearance of the one thing he shared with his father. The truth is, my dad and I never talked much. Ours was not a relationship based on games of catch and walks in the woods, of man-to-man talks and scout camp. Art was really the only area in which we collaborated, and we had lost to Tinkertoys, Lincoln Logs, and Yakov Golnick's father.

At any rate, after the menorah competition, I remember only one other time when I called on my father's artistry to bail me out. I was in a high school history class, and my teacher, Mr. Alan Mumbrue, had xeroxed blank maps of the United States, upon which we were supposed to draw various items of historical or geographical significance. On one map, we were to draw bodies of water; on another, trails. And so on. I had procrastinated work on the assignment, and the night before it was due, I realized that I had left the blank maps in my locker at school. At which point, after observing my panic, my dad offered to draw me a map of the United States; he did it freehand on posterboard in less than hour. I stayed up past midnight drawing trails, rivers, and railroad lines, and delivered the map on time to Mr. Mumbruc, who promptly rewarded me with a C for using posterboard instead of the blank maps he had provided.

As for my father, he seemed to become less and less interested in art as the years drew on. The large-scale projects were a thing of the past. His backyard fountain remained unfinished, stored in its barium barrel. He no longer took photographs with his Exakta camera or movies with his Super 8. The only times he would draw were when my mother or sister would coax him into doing so for a birthday or some other celebration, but even then, his heart rarely seemed in the process. Shortly after I graduated from college, I took a trip to Europe with my brother. In Paris, we bought our father one hundred colored pencils and a sketchpad, but I don't believe he ever used them. Whether this was because of the beginnings of arthritis or for some more profound existential reason, the novelist in me might have an idea or two, but the son really cannot say.

Eventually, after he retired from medical practice, my father did begin to draw again — the view out our front window on Mozart Street, his own arms and hands. Most of what he drew were memories of a life that had ended long before I was born; over and over, he drew with what seemed to be crystal clarity his father's old pop factory on Thirty-ninth and Drexel and the S & L Beverages' delivery truck, which was, I guess you might say, his way of staring at a snow globe and saying, "Rosebud."

> **It was my first Chanukah as a father, my first Chanukah without a father.**

A little more than a month and a half after my father passed away, at the age of eighty, my wife and I spent our first Chanukah with our seven-month-old daughter. We gathered around one of our back windows; I lit the *shamash,* said the *brachot* over the candles, and sang the Chanukah songs that I remembered from Hebrew school — "Maoz Tzur," "Dreidel Mine (Spin Spin Spin)," "Who Can Retell (the Things That Befell Us)." It was my first Chanukah as a father, my first Chanukah without a father.

Not long after that Chanukah night, I was talking on the phone to my mother. She said that she had been considering buying my brother and his family a menorah for Chanukah, but that he had told her he didn't need one because he was making his own. What was he using to make it, I asked.

"Tinfoil," said my mother.

An Israeli Chanukah

I T IS A COLD DECEMBER MORNING IN ISRAEL, AND ALTHOUGH IT IS DARK IN MY ROOM FROM THE *TRISSIM,* THE BLACKOUT WARTIME SHADES, I KNOW IT IS LIGHT OUT, DESPITE THE RAIN PELTING AT MY WINDOW LIKE BULLETS: *RAT-TAT-TAT, RAT-TAT-TAT.* STEADY AND SURE, AS IF WINTER WILL LAST FOREVER.

The air is chilly and I am loath to slip my naked feet onto the frigid *balatot,* the marble tiles that are also a signature of every Jerusalem home, by regulation built out of white stone and floored with ugly speckled squares.

The radio shrieks on, bleeping eight piercing whistles to signify the news: "Kol Israel, shalom, it's eight o' clock, Sunday morning, December twenty-fifth, and here is the news . . ."

Oh God. I have to get out of bed. It's Sunday. Sunday: a working day. Sunday is a workday in Israel. I'll never get used to this, I think, but still I run out of bed and into the shower, all thoughts of cold escaping me as I hurry to get to the office, to sneak in there without anyone noticing that I am late again, hurrying to get to my work so it'll look as if I've been doing it furiously all morning.

Which is why I don't realize until much later in the day, until after I've sufficiently pounded through my work like a robot on speed, what today is. Besides Sunday. It's Sunday, December 25. Christmas.

Here we're nearing the end of Chanukah, but the rest of the world is just waking up to open presents. They are decking the halls with boughs of holly, celebrating the birth of Jesus, or twelve days of shopping or being home with the family or whatever it is people do when they celebrate Christmas. The thing is, I have no real clue.

Even though I'm twenty-five years old, I don't know much about Christmas except what I've seen on TV or in movies or in store window displays. I grew up in Brooklyn, New York, and all my relatives, friends, teachers, and even acquaintances were Orthodox Jews, or some maybe just Conservative Jews but religious nonetheless. No one I knew celebrated Christmas. And I mean *no one*. I'd heard of Jews who had "Chanukah bushes" or even Christmas trees, but those might have been urban legends, fabricated cautionary tales. Who knew if they were even true?

Not I. When I was growing up, December was for Chanukah. Like most of the families on the block, we placed our menorahs in the front window in order to publicize the miracle of the Temple oil that lasted for eight days instead of one, of the God that helped a small Jewish nation win the war against the powerful Hellenists.

Our menorahs stood on a rickety, old wheeled stand covered in tinfoil, tinfoil that was covered in globs of colored candle tears. By the eighth day of the holiday, our window front was ablaze in a haze of forty-five candles, a testament to the individuality of our religion, where each of us got our own menorah. My father had his oil lamp,

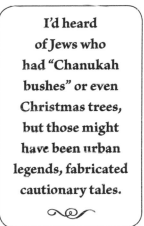

I'd heard of Jews who had "Chanukah bushes" or even Christmas trees, but those might have been urban legends, fabricated cautionary tales.

the only one that was technically kosher, since the oil burned for an hour, as decreed by Jewish law. While he surgically squirted oil into the glass bulbs, then clumsily tried to thread the short wicks with his thick fingers, we four children squabbled over which candles to use.

"I am *not* using green," I would say, throwing the puke-colored candles over to my poor younger brother, the fourth behind three color-conscious girls. My older sister might do red, white, and blue, for America, so maybe I'd do blue and white, for Israel. Another night she'd do pink, orange, and red, just to flash her flair for fashion. Someone, some night, would have to use all the green candles just to get rid of the remainders, an act of charity.

We each lit our masterpieces, said the blessings aloud, and then sang Hebrew songs, jaunty tunes about war and victory, with multiple harmonies and duets. First the traditional "Maoz Tzur," God is Our Rock, followed by "Mi Yimallel": Who Will Speak the Powers of Israel?

Then we'd pile into the living room for an hour while the candles burned, to play dreidel; or, if my father was in the mood, he'd show us how to play marbles, like he did when he was a kid. Actually, our Chanukah, in the 1970s and '80s, was really something out of the 1950s, an anachronistic re-creation of his era. We all got Chanukah gelt — money — instead of presents, like the other kids in my class. Year after year, despite our complaints, we still received cash, not even one dinky gift. (Some kids got eight, one for each night!)

"Presents are for Christmas, not Chanukah," my father insisted, and he still does, to this day.

But that's how Chanukah was in the recesses of religious Brooklyn, far away from Christmas trees and Christmas carolers and midnight Mass. It was still defined by what it was not: Christmas.

That's why the move to Israel was so refreshing for me. All Jewish holidays, all the time.

A week after my college graduation, I took off for the promised land. I figured if I was going to lead a sheltered life — with only Jews, for only Jews — I might as well do it in a Jewish state. A Jewish state whose national holidays are Rosh Hashanah, Sukkot, Passover, and Chanukah. In Israel, on the Jewish holidays schools are closed, and businesses often are too. Trips are taken, families gather together for a meal or two and possibly, although not usually, a religious experience.

While Israel is primarily a secular country, everyone celebrates the religious holidays, often in a watered-down way (much the way Americans celebrate Christian holidays). The Passover Seder is a boozy meal with traditional foods and readings; the High Holidays are an excuse for family, apples, and honey; and Sukkot is for nature lovers, with overnight camping trips to the desert and the lush north. And Chanukah?

Chanukah is a different kind of festival, probably because it's the one of the few that can't be celebrated with a barbecue. (If there's sunshine and a day off in Israel, it's time to bring out the burgers.) Hiking is probably out of the question, too. So the main tradition that's left? Food, of course.

By early December every kiosk and supermarket has set up a presentation of open cardboard boxes filled with an array of fresh, sumptuous doughnuts. Not exactly doughnuts. *Sufganiyot:*

a mound of powdered dough, with jelly, cream, caramel, or choc-olate filling gushing out like a geyser (often from the wrong end). *Sufganiyot,* like potato latkes, are fried, in order to celebrate the miracle of the oil lasting eight days.

In the center of town a giant electric menorah is "lit" every night. Throngs of powder-faced teenagers gorging on doughnuts wander through the *midrachov,* the cobblestoned pedestrian square closed to traffic, until way past their bedtime — but there is no bedtime, because it's Chanukah vacation.

After we traipse through town, my roommate and I go home and light her menorah: each candleholder depicts a synagogue from around the world. We live in a small, two-bedroom apart-ment centrally located in the fairly Americanized Jerusalem neighborhood called Katamon.

For us, Chanukah unearths a debate that's been going on for centuries. Yes, I'm talking potato latkes: grated or mashed?

My grandmother always peeled her potatoes, then processed them into a puree. She pan-fried the latkes on the stove in a swimming pool of vegetable oil. The latkes were thin at the edges and gooey in the middle, the insides salty and smooth, like baby food.

But my roommate, a budding chef from California, came from a long line of graters. Her latkes are also fried, but they are supple and stringy, the potato strands intertwined like pieces of a puzzle.

In the end, my roommate makes both kinds, and adds a sweet-potato variation, filling the counters with bowls of potato glop, trying to get them into the pan before they turn brown from sitting out. For days to come our apartment, our clothes, our hair, and even our books will smell like latkes, but we don't think about that as all our friends come over to sample the fare. And a yearly party is born. My room-

> **Chanukah unearths a debate that's been going on for centuries. Yes, I'm talking potato latkes: grated or mashed?**

mate and I move to a larger, three-bedroom apartment, still in an American neighborhood, and invite the expatriate community for more than a latkes tasting. Fifty or sixty or seventy people arrive — Americans, Brits, Australians, South Africans, and a few French and Belgians to shake it up — and they come to expect the party each year — a tradition, like lighting the menorah.

Now that I'm not in my father's house anymore, and now that I'm not near the American frenzy of gift giving, I feel it's fine to give gifts on Chanukah. Why not? Our party has a grab bag, where each person brings a small tchotchke — a Krazy Straw, a yo-yo, a Super Ball — nothing that anyone would ever need, which is why half the gifts are left at our house on Saturday night.

Which is why I'm late to work on Sunday morning, because I've stayed up till three A.M. hosting Chanukah guests. On

December 24, no less. Funny to think it was Christmas Eve. It was just another Saturday night in Jerusalem.

And now it's just another Sunday, a working day for me. Christmas is almost over, and it's a relief — liberating, actually — to have almost missed it.

It's only years later that I realize the irony: I've moved to Jesus's birthplace — I live just twenty minutes from Bethlehem, maybe an hour from Nazareth — to avoid the celebration of his birth, his life.

But I suppose this is one of the reasons I moved to Israel. No, in essence, it *is* the reason I moved to Israel. To be surrounded by my culture, to live in the majority culture.

In America, despite all the politically correct inclusiveness, "holiday" means "Christmas," and Chanukah is relegated to being *Not That Holiday*. In Israel Chanukah isn't *That Holiday*, because there hardly is another holiday. There are no TV spots wishing people a benign "Season's Greetings," to include everyone's holidays, even newer holidays, like Kwanzaa; in Israel there are only "Happy Chanukah" ads on television because that's the only holiday there is.

It's not really all there is. People know about Christmas here. It's called Chag Ha'molad, the Holiday of the Birth, obliquely referring to the action, not the man. (They also call New Year's Eve Sylvester, like the Germans do, although Israelis probably don't know it's named for Saint Sylvester, who was pope in the fourth century C.E. and allegedly cured Constantine from leprosy, after converting him to Christianity.)

Cable channels run *It's a Wonderful Life* and *Frosty the Snowman,* which must leave Israelis scratching their heads — what is this obsession with snow? We American expats watch nostalgically (although there must be another word for feeling nostalgia for a holiday you never had . . .).

And people do celebrate: thousands of tourists come in to be baptized in the Jordan River, go to midnight Mass in Bethlehem, tour the churches of Nazareth.

But for most of my seven years in Israel, I'm oblivious to Christmas and all its accompaniments.

Which is why it is such a shock for me to leave.

I leave for the summer, temporarily, but summer ends and fall begins and suddenly it is Thanksgiving and I am still in America. The radio is driving me crazy with Christmas songs, TV commercials blast ads for the best Christmas sales, and a mad spell is cast over New York City, as if, in a variation on *Invasion of the Body Snatchers,* all the inhabitants have been infected with the incorrigible urge to shop, shop, shop.

After seven years in Israel, I find the sight of so many stores and material goods overwhelming, especially with the advent of superstores like Costco (which could feed and clothe the entire nation of Israel, if not the Palestinians too). I come to learn that "shopping" is an activity one can spend an entire day — or week! — on, which is what everyone seems to be doing for . . . Christmas.

Okay, so it's not really the shopping that bothers me, but the sensation that there's a giant party to which everyone else but me is invited: the Christmas celebration. I no longer live in Brooklyn, solely among Orthodox Jews, and now I see how the other half lives: there are office holiday parties and media holiday parties and friends' holiday parties, all with giant evergreens in the center of the room and mistletoe hanging in every other doorway. Sure, there's a table with a lonely little menorah surrounded by a couple of puny gold chocolates and pink and purple plastic driedels, but it's off to the side, almost invisible, dwarfed by the glittering gold and blue and green ornaments and lights hanging from the tree. Christmas is everywhere. And Chanukah is, once again, *Not That Holiday.*

> **It's not really the shopping that bothers me, but the sensation that there's a giant party to which everyone else but me is invited.**

Those were my feelings my first year back here. I've been here seven now, and I've come to accept the reordering of things. Friday is now a workday, Sunday a day off. January is the New Year and September is only the High Holidays. And come November — the minute Halloween is over, it seems — those Christmas songs will be playing on the radio.

I've learned not to let Chanukah be pushed off to the side of the dance floor. I still throw huge Chanukah parties, where people bring grab-bag prizes and eat (store-bought) latkes and doughnuts. I light the menorah each night with friends and sing the same jaunty tunes of childhood. Because it's different for me now, this time around in America. I revel in my Chanukah joys because I know that halfway around the world, come December, people are celebrating Chanukah like there's no other holiday. Because Chanukah is the only holiday there is.

Presents!

THE YEAR I WAS NINE, MY FATHER AND I DID THE FIRST NIGHT OF CHANUKAH AT THE STEINS' HOUSE ON THE UPPER WEST SIDE. MELISSA STEIN WAS ELEVEN AND ABOUT TWENTY POUNDS HEAVIER THAN ME. AFTER DINNER AND BEFORE PRESENTS, WE WENT TO HER BEDROOM AND PLAYED A GAME ON HER BED CALLED DRIVE THE CAR. I GOT UP ON TOP OF HER AND WORKED the stick shift, which I think was her elbow, and pushed the pedals, which were her knees. The car, which was her, got going faster and faster, and then there was the accident once we really had some speed going, where the car suddenly turned all wobbly and then everything broke and the car lay flat and whirring. I fell on top of the smashed car and there we were,

> That's what
> Chanukah is for me:
> scrambling around,
> trying to get my fair
> share of presents
> and sex.
>
> ⌁⌁

hugging or whatever, fucking around without being able to take it anywhere, since we were children. I remember liking the game and hoping that I might play it with girls from school who I liked better than Melissa Stein, who was just my dad's friend from college's kid who went to private school and was kind of snobby when she wasn't letting me climb all over her.

Then we got called into the living room for flourless chocolate cake and the first Chanukah present. I got a record player from my dad and he said, That's it. That's all you get. I said, What about the next seven gifts? And he was like, You got the eight gifts right here: there's a speaker, and another speaker, and the turntable, and the needle, and the volume control, and the on and off switch, et cetera. The Steins laughed and laughed. So that's what Chanukah is for me: scrambling around, trying to get my fair share of presents and sex.

GROWING UP, I didn't have crushes on Jewish girls, because after my parents got divorced my dad didn't really go for the Jewish ladies. Now I'm married to a Quaker. We have a menorah somewhere, I don't know where, but I'm going to have to fight to use it with our kids, assuming we have some, which is another thing I'm praying about. My wife is a lot younger than I am, and in my weak moments I suspect she'll leave me for some more upbeat guy, some robust Christian with a lot of earning power who doesn't spend Friday nights brooding about how he has no friends but instead takes time to plan fun adventures where they pack a picnic lunch and go climb a little mountain and make sure to take their garbage with them, their napkins and plastic wrap and knives for the pâté and whatever, when they climb back down. Actually, I'd like to marry that guy, too. And during the hike if I bring up Chanukah and my marginally Jewish upbringing, which was fueled mostly by loneliness and despair and arrogance, he can tell me to shut up and tie my hiking boots tighter and maybe move a little quicker too, huh? Because life is about more than just wanting presents and we're trying to make it up this mountain and back down before the sun sets and we all catch colds. And what about giving back to the group, anyway? He'd want to know about that and I'd have to admit that no, I'm still trying to learn about the power of giving.

MY MOM CARED even less for organized religion than my dad did. She gave me her copy of *The Wanderers* by Richard Price for Chanukah, because she felt bad that my dad had played a joke on me with that record player. I remember not bothering with that book until the summer, when I read it one afternoon on a swing at someone's country house on Long Island. We never had a country house — not that we couldn't have afforded one, we totally could have, but since my parents were divorced neither of them could be bothered. So most times that are naturally happy for people, vacation times, were shit for me, since I was alone reading. Too bad for my wife, huh? Anyway, my mom gave me *The Wanderers*, a book that mattered to me in a different way than better stuff, like the requisite group of books by Philip Roth that every boy should read. But *The Wanderers* was a book that I read before I understood what it was about, so when one character asks "Do you have any bags?" when they're about to have sex with a girl at their friend's house, I thought they meant brown paper bags, so they could come in the bags. Yep, didn't realize till a lot later that they meant condoms. I guess I looked forward to next Chanukah, when I'd hop off Melissa Stein and dash around her bedroom, desperately looking for a brown paper bag before I made a mess.

Around that same time, I read *Ladies' Man* by Richard Price, which I snagged from my mom at my grandparents' house one holiday season back when Chanukah came at the same time as Christmas, so this must've been around 1980. That's the most depressing book in the whole world, where the main character is losing his girlfriend, who he calls La Di, and it's the seventies, and everybody in New York wants to just die because they're singing the same song La Di sings at her audition, which just ruins everything. That song was — you guessed it — "Feelings."

I DID USE that record player, and I appreciated it. I just wish my father hadn't played a joke on me. Or maybe it would've been better if I was less spoiled? I remember going out to dinner with my dad and a friend of his to an Indian restaurant. They ordered and then the waitress looked at me and smiled and I said, I'll have the grand taster's platter for two! My dad just shook his head and said, Like hell you will. But I was going to share it, I said. I don't think you know how to share yet, my father said. And he was right. So I got the chicken tandoori and brooded. I knew I was spoiled and had an attitude problem, but I was an only child and couldn't help myself.

I bought Who records to play on that record player and, specifically, *Tommy*, a record that I bought with Chanukah gelt and played exactly once. I got terribly freaked out when Tommy gets his balls fondled while he plays a mean pinball and I wrapped the record back up in its plastic and got my babysitter, this lesbian named Seal who worked in a plant shop called the Enchanted Garden and who used to deal pot to her friends in front of me, to take me down to Sound Track on Seventh Avenue in Park Slope, Brooklyn, to return it. I bought *Led Zeppelin III* instead. I didn't understand that record at all, either. But I liked playing with the pinwheel. Yeah, that was the end of the seventies in Brooklyn, and Chanukah didn't mean much to me since I was such an avaricious kid, but classic rock and sex were huge presences that barely left room for anything else. That's how I began to process Chanukah: it was the time when you get some presents and a very special gypped feeling that you're a Jew and always will be and you'll never get to join in the reindeer games, especially if you're an only child who doesn't know how to share with others.

My Grandmother Bea is ninety-one and my Aunt Dee is sixty-something and my wife and I were hanging out one Sunday recently at about five in the afternoon in West Orange, New Jersey, at my grandmother's condominium. We'd finished up our portions of egg salad and tuna fish on challah bread and we were just talking. Maybe we were eating some orange slices and Hershey's Kisses and listening to the air conditioner. Maybe we finished up with some of those individually wrapped coffee-nips candies. So I was like, Chanukah, right? And Dee was like, Oh yeah, that's bullshit if there ever was bullshit. Though of course she didn't curse like that. But she was like, Kwanzaa for the Jews, no doubt! In 1955 we weren't getting eight presents! Nuh-uh. Rather, it was yet another incidental holiday that didn't hold a candle to the high ones or even Pesach, yeah, the holidays that matter to the real Jews. And I noted how I grew up twisted on

> It was the time when you get some presents and a very special gypped feeling that you're a Jew and always will be and you'll never get to join in the reindeer games.

the pyre of this cultural goof of a holiday, this holiday that had me totally feeding into my materialistic side. And my grandmother and my aunt and my wife said, Well, that's not our problem that you're an asshole like that.

MY WIFE AND I are going to butt heads for sure about having the tree in the house when we have kids, and we'll most definitely be doing her family traditions because they actually make her happy, like the gingerbread house made out of graham crackers at Christmas (the graham crackers are the gingerbread-house equivalent of drywall) and she'll put them in a nonreligious context. Thank G–d. Because she's ambivalent or atheistic or both on G–d, but deeply committed to the concept of tradition. Because she believes tradition makes people happy! And now, finally, I understand that she's right. It's good to have somewhere to go and some other folks to be with during a time when you can't go to work and be yourself and you also can't lie on your side and just read a book, and it's especially nice to have something to do when you get there, like open presents!

I'm starting to like tradition. One of the great things about becoming an adult is that I understand what's great about being a Jew. But I can't stop with the presents. I love presents, and if we could just get some kids going I'm sure I'd like to give them some presents almost as much I'd like to get more presents for me. There's so much stuff I'm going to get as soon as I have more money, like a pair of Gallo Reference 1 loudspeakers, a McIntosh preamp and amp, one of those fiftieth-anniversary Eames chairs (I really do not care that it's a cliché. Those things can put you to sleep faster than Xanax) and some of those New Balance 992s in black and maybe a houndstooth suit from Paul Stuart and some Crockett & Jones suede shoes and an IWC Mark XII watch. Yeah, that's some stuff I want for Chanukah, along with a car, but not a German car. Nope, do not take me there. I'll probably have kids, and that will keep me from being able to afford all that stuff. But that'll be okay, because it'll be nice to get the kids some things. And maybe we'll have a menorah we can set up on a counter in the kitchen or something, so they'll remember that Dad is Jewish, after all, and a little part of them is, too.

KAREN E. BENDER AND
ROBERT ANTHONY SIEGEL

The Light, the Sword, and the Nintendo DS

THE MACCABEES DIDN'T STAND A CHANCE AGAINST THE CATALOGS THAT BEGAN TO APPEAR IN MID-NOVEMBER. OUR CHILDREN, JONAH AND MAIA, BEGAN TO LOOK THROUGH THEM AS A HOBBY. THEY EACH SETTLED ON ONE EXPENSIVE PRESENT THAT WOULD LINK THEIR LONGING WITH THAT OF A GAZILLION OTHER CHILDREN, JEWISH AND CHRISTIAN, A terrifying and determined mob, plotting their conquests around the globe. We dreaded the arrival of the catalogs each afternoon. The children could spot them sticking out of our mailbox like eagles spotting a mouse from a great height. They were their Torahs, their holy books.

"I get to see it first!" Jonah, who was six, screamed.

"No, me!" Maia, who was two, shrieked.

Jonah could read his electronics catalog by himself, and did so with a strange sort of tenderness, as if learning for the first time of the world's bounty. "Good news, Dad," he said, when we went to tuck him in for the night. "Nintendo DS comes with a game bundle, and it's only a hundred and forty-nine dollars!" He seemed genuinely glad — not for himself only but for us, that this miracle was possible.

Maia still needed a little help, however. She would sit cross-legged on the floor with her *American Girl* catalog on her lap and say, "Read!" with that threatening look on her face that pre-saged an explosion. We would spend what seemed to be interminable, eerie hours reading aloud the text accompanying pictures of scarily vapid, saccharine dolls in period costumes, until we could simply recite the words by heart. Maia would caress the pictures as we spoke, staring with longing as if recalling a long-lost love. Over time, we noticed that there was one picture in particular to which she kept returning: Marisol, a girl in a purple tutu. "Is Marisol the one you want?" we asked.

Maia nodded shyly.

"Then you will get Marisol."

Maia jumped up and began doing a genuine dance of joy, waving her hands over her head and swaying, her delicate face radiant with pleasure. The price tag: only $87 with a jazzy girl outfit; $26 more for the tutu.

This wasn't exactly what we had intended. When we'd had our children, we'd wanted to improve upon our own experience, to give them the holiday experience that we now wished we had had. While we had, as a young married couple, celebrated Chanukah carelessly, whenever we saw fit, we now wanted to know exactly when Chanukah fell; we wanted to know what the letters on the dreidel meant. Suddenly, as parents, we were the ones who could construct the world that would help our children create their own memories.

Plus, while we had been raised in the cities of Los Angeles and New York, among two of the most concentrated Jewish populations on the globe, our children were being raised in Wilmington, North Carolina, where our son was the only Jewish child in his entire elementary school. During the month of December, houses everywhere became artistic tributes to various forms of Santa; our next-door neighbor had designed a Santa out of potato sacks, plopped him on top of a tractor,

> **Our children were being raised in Wilmington, North Carolina, where our son was the only Jewish child in his entire elementary school.**

and parked this odd creation in front of his house. Our house was the only one on the block that was dark.

We had bought our first menorah at a sale by the Ladies Concordia Society at the Temple of Israel, the Reform temple that we had joined soon after arriving in Wilmington. We had been surprised by the variety of items and tchotchkes on sale. There were menorahs with ceramic sports figures, with Disney characters, and a military one featuring metal replicas of tanks. There were Chanukah doodads of astounding variety: bags of gelt, but also a bag of jelly beans called "Maccabeans," a yo-yo with a menorah on it that played "I Have a Little Dreidel" when you tossed it, electric dreidels that bounced, kits where you could roll your own beeswax candles, Chanukah finger puppets, coloring books, and so on. We loaded up. We would create our own version of Chanukah for our children. But what would it be?

Our Chanukah would focus not on the presents, which we'd learned was a recent innovation to compete against Christmas, but instead on the story that the holiday was meant to celebrate: the victory of the Maccabees against King Antiochus, who tried to suppress the Jewish religion, and the miracle of the Temple light.

Needless to say, the children had never really cooperated in that venture. It didn't help matters that Chanukah is a relatively minor holiday in the Jewish tradition. Yes, a successful revolt, men with spears, a guy named "The Hammer," but what it all comes down to is *oil that lasts longer than expected.* Ultimately, that is a tough sell to two children in a small southern city temporarily inundated with images of wise men with camels, drummer boys, talking animals in a manger, a fat man in a red suit who hands out gifts for free, and something they can really identify with: a baby his parents think is God.

Jonah was two when he began to notice the Christmas frenzy going on around him and started throwing tantrums in front of department store windows, having breakdowns at friends' houses when he saw all the new toys they had scored, and asking confused questions about Santa Claus and where this incredible bounty of bleeping, whirring, flashing goodies came from.

Rather than being an expression of our Jewish identity, Chanukah very quickly became the thing that would protect us from the evils of Christmas. To an extent it worked: we didn't have to haul him out of the mall kicking and screaming — or not all the time, anyway — and we didn't have to worry about him converting to Christianity each December. Every time he saw one of those Santa shows on TV — the kind that seem to function as infomercials for some hidden cabal of toy manufacturers — we could just say, "Forget about Christmas. You get Chanukah, you lucky dog, and it lasts for eight days instead of just one! Tell that to your little gentile friends!"

Of course, this did not really address the greed problem. If anything, it made it worse; we were essentially signaling to our children that they would find a better rate of return in being Jewish than Christian. So while we were disturbed and frightened by the greed we had unleashed, we were nevertheless captive to it, and telling them once again about the Maccabees was beginning to feel futile. "So you see," we said, "the greatest miracle of them all was the decision to light the lamp, not knowing whether the oil would last — the miracle of hope."

"Can I get the enhanced game bundle?" asked Jonah.

"And I want tutu!" said Maia.

"Don't you understand?" we asked. "If Judah Maccabee hadn't beaten the Romans, we would be praying to Zeus right now."

Jonah thought about this. "Does he give toys too?"

THIS TIME, WE told the children that they would get all their presents on the first night, after dinner and the lighting of the candles. The idea was that taking care of the gift giving right away would leave the rest of the holiday free of greed. After some arguing it was decided that the schedule could be moved up — we would open presents before dinner, though after the candles . . . well, before the candles. . . . It was midafternoon and still light out when they began ripping furiously at the wrapping. It was like watch-

> "Can I get the enhanced game bundle?" asked Jonah.

ing piranhas feed. We stood by stunned and a little frightened, waiting for the joy that would be our reward.

We moved closer to Maia as she began to unwrap the American Girl doll that she had pointed to in the catalog again and again. Marisol. We had ordered Marisol on December 1, as supplies were limited, and the customer service agent had said that Marisol was on back order but was guaranteed to arrive by December 25, which was now happily the first night of Chanukah.

"Maia, here's Marisol," we said. She lifted Marisol out of the box and placed her on her lap.

There was silence.

"I hate her," said Maia.

"What?" we asked, realizing, with horror, that she was not wearing the tutu she had worn in the catalog.

"Not right doll!" shrieked Maia and threw the doll across the room.

It did not go well with the Princess Alexa carriage, either, which we opened and found in many pieces, with instructions so complex they might as well have been for a spacecraft. Maia stood by the disassembled pieces and wailed, "Where my carriage?"

Jonah tore open the Nintendo he had been pleading for, which we had once caught him murmuring about in his dreams ("comes with Mario for one forty-nine"). He had never seen the thing before, but he was caught in a kind of trance as he instantly found the on button, pushed it, and began playing, as though simply resuming a game that had been interrupted in some past life. "Jonah, do you like it?" we asked him. He stared at the screen, mouth open. We watched, forgotten.

We sat, disappointed by the children's reactions. Or maybe "disappointed" was not the word — we'd been cheated. We had hoped that our generosity would make our children turn to us with renewed love and faith in the world's goodness. Instead, they'd had the bad manners to either protest or ignore us. What was this? What had happened to the joy of Chanukah?

As with any riot, the roots of our Chanukah conflagration lay in the past — or should we say in Chanukahs past? We adults had each had different experiences with the holiday.

Karen:

In my family, the Chanukah presents were given on one night, with much fanfare. The menorah was lit, the prayer said, but the latkes were always frozen, no one really knew how to play with a dreidel, and nobody retold the story of the Maccabees or the Temple light. The presents from the chorus of relatives were arranged on the fireplace, in towers organized by name.

My sisters and I were urged, or perhaps required, to make presents for the relatives, not buy them. It was a large group, not all particularly deserving of a homemade present, but there they were. Chanukah was associated with a factory in the bedroom, glue, glitter, overuse of the word *love*, spelling of *Chanukah* on homemade cards in various ways, made-up piano compositions that I had to play for everyone, individualized tributes to aunts, uncles, grandparents. It was exhausting. It was not always sincere. Once I rebelled and bought a package of pink soaps shaped like roses at a drugstore for my mother; it was a huge relief. Regular consumers seemed distant, glamorous figures who could go into a store, plunk down some money, and, with that simple action, be absolved.

When I grew up, Chanukah became absorbed into the current of blind festivity that was December. It was a chance for me to unload dozens of homemade mini – pumpkin breads onto friends and relatives, having moved from homemade cards to baked goods; it was a chance to visit relatives; but I frequently did not know what days Chanukah actually fell on.

Robert:

In contrast, my childhood Chanukahs were marked by near-Dionysian excess, and the sort of heavy-laden, self-disgusted feeling that I would know later in life on New Year's morning, stumbling home at early dawn. My parents would hide presents every night and we would scurry around the apartment to find them, and when we did, we would tear at the wrappers like madmen. We spent no time playing with these toys, however, because we were too busy fighting about who'd gotten the better present, or wondering what the next night's haul would bring, or badgering our parents to reveal what was coming, or, once that had finally been revealed, angling for something even better. The atmosphere in the house was feverish, hallucinatory. But the strangest thing was that it didn't just happen by accident: no, our parents actually *liked* orchestrating this frenzy. One Chanukah, we hit the eight-day mark, ran out of candleholders on the menorah, and were all so reluctant to come down off the love binge that we just kept going: the pattern of hiding, finding, and complaining repeated each night for twenty-two nights, till we were burnt out and nerve-dead, our rooms piled with toys we had absolutely no interest in.

> **The truth was that I knew only Greedikah, not Chanukah.**

As an adult, living on my own, I found that the holiday brought up vaguely troubling associations, and I ignored it. The truth was that I knew only Greedikah, not Chanukah, and I wasn't greedy for *things* anymore.

THE SIGHT OF Maia throwing Marisol across a room littered with shredded wrapping paper and other very expensive toys in various states of disassemblage and nonappreciation was shocking enough to lead us to a resolution: we were tired of celebrating Greedikah. The kids would have to learn the true meaning of Chanukah, even if it killed us (or them). And so we threw ourselves into Chanukah as a project. Each night, we had a different activity. We made latkes by hand, grating the potatoes, throwing them into the bubbling oil. We went to a friend's big Chanukah party — with fifty people, perhaps the largest Chanukah party in the city.

We tried to tell them the story. "How would you feel," we asked Jonah at breakfast the next morning, "if someone said you couldn't play soccer?" He was wide-eyed; we could see that we were reaching him. We tried to think of his version of a holy book. "How would you feel if someone said you couldn't read *Captain Underpants*?"

He nodded gravely. "I'd feel really bad if someone said I couldn't have my Nintendo."

Was this it? Was it close? "Well, yeah, that's it. That's sort of how the Maccabees felt, sort of."

What was the Chanukah story, exactly? We read the children's versions we had bought for them. It had everything, frankly, that children would like. Unfair rules. Rebellion. Battles. Magical fire.

We played up the battle part.

"Then Judah the Maccabee spurred the Jews to take back the Temple!"

We learned the dreidel game and played it with pennies;

somehow, Jonah figured out how to twist the dreidel, or turn it, so it landed on *gimel* and he always won. He exulted, perhaps not unlike Judah the Maccabee.

"I am Jonah the Maccabee, king of dreidels!" he proclaimed.

We talked about the oil. "What if your Nintendo was losing its charge," we suggested, "but it kept going. And going. For days. It still worked."

He stared at us; he was listening.

We spent a night rolling candles made from strips of beeswax. Jonah and Maia stood still at the table, watching the flames. There was an appealing pyromaniacal aspect to Chanukah. There was one flame, then two, then three. There was something basic and mesmerizing about the flames, something so superior, we felt, to the gaudy ornamentation of a Christmas tree. The simple spectacle of the row of light. We did not necessarily feel a connection to anything miraculous but, instead, a sort of breathlessness, the understanding that the Maccabees, whoever they were, had watched flames just like this in a ruined temple twenty-two hundred years ago.

> There was an appealing pyromaniacal aspect to Chanukah.

The fifth night, Jonah asked if he could light the candles.

"He can," said his grandmother, and we looked at her, aghast — a seven-year-old armed with a *shamash*, a tiny torch? But Jonah looked as though his own miraculousness had finally been acknowledged. We lit a candle and handed it to him.

We said the prayer, and Jonah slowly, carefully, lit each candle.

"Let's turn off the lights!" Jonah suggested.

We did. The candles glowed in the darkness.

"Let's watch them melt," he said.

We were quiet. The flames rose up, watery, pale, in the dark kitchen. We watched them melt.

Then our son told us the Chanukah story. He told about the Greeks who told the Jews they would have to worship the Greek gods. "They said, *You can't worship any gods but ours!*" he said with gusto, clenching his fist. He described how the great Temple was ruined and how, when the Maccabees entered it, they had only one night of oil. He knew it all. He told the story of what had happened thousands of years ago slowly, like a miniature rabbi. The way he told it, it was a good story. It was the fifth night of Chanukah. He was seven years old. We sat in the darkness, the light on our faces, and listened to him.

Eight Nights

Night One

THE FIRST CHANUKAH THAT YOU REMEMBER CLEARLY IS SPENT AT YOUR GRANDPARENTS' GARDEN APARTMENT IN BROOKLYN, NEW YORK. NEAR THE COLLEGE THAT STARTS WITH A *B*. NEAR AN AVENUE THAT STARTS WITH THE LETTER *R*. YOU ARE THREE AND A HALF YEARS OLD. LETTERS ARE A VERY BIG DEAL.

There are steps leading out to the garden and your grandparents have strewn blue and gold lights along the railing, like little beams. And your gifts are lined up, like promises, on the kitchen table. It doesn't occur to you to open them — what could be inside that is as good as the pretty pink paper? The lacy ribbons? Your grandfather swoops you on his lap (because you lose him young, he will always be this to you: all arms and laughter and smiles). The two of you sit quietly while your grandma works on the crossword puzzle. It is Sunday. She works quickly and seriously. You like watching the way her hand moves with the pen. And when you reach out to touch her, knocking the pen, she smiles at you.

Night Two

In the white-brick Hebrew school—in the back of the white-brick temple—you sit in a circle with the rest of the class and someone—not the head teacher but the teacher's assistant, the one you get to call by his first name, the one you call Peter or Paul or Gilligan—explains to you why it is important to light the candles, why it is important to do it a certain way. He explains that putting the menorah by the window has everything to do with lighting the outside world, as opposed to just illuminating your own house. It has everything to do with sharing the miracle of Chanukah.

Someone snickers at the word *miracle.* You are a classroom full of fifth graders. Someone is always snickering at the world *miracle.*

You all head to the windowsill, where

> **He explains that putting the menorah by the window has everything to do with lighting the outside world, as opposed to just illuminating your own house.**

the menorah will stay, and you hold out your hand and wait for your turn to light one. You care that you do it well, but you are also aware of Sara and Jennifer whispering on the other side of the circle. You wish they were whispering to you too. Which makes you think you shouldn't be worrying so much about the candles. You should worry about other things instead—things that girls your age worry about. What are those things? Boys? No. They scare you, now that they might actually try to kiss you. Nail polish? Basketball? You aren't sure. It is one of your first reminders that you aren't always very good at being you.

Are you ready, Gilligan asks you, handing over a candle. He says it in a way that indicates that it isn't the first time he is asking you. Somehow you have missed it.

You look at Jennifer. I hope so, you say.

Night Three

A snowstorm, three months after your brother has left for his freshman year of college. You aren't supposed to miss him—certainly haven't planned on such a thing—but something has switched between you in his absence. He calls you on the telephone, like it is something that you do. He asks you what you did that day—asks about junior high school, your teachers there. He knows their names. It is your first Chanukah without him.

Since your mother is away too, it feels like ample evidence that the candles don't need to be lit. You are thirteen years old.

You are always looking for evidence that you don't need to do something.

When you present your case to your dad, you can tell he is apt to agree (he is a lawyer; he likes evidence too) but he tells you that your mom would want you two to light them, so you follow him (or maybe he follows you) into the dining room — with its long table and formal place settings. In your entire life, you have spent approximately one hour in the dining room with the long table and formal place settings.

You are wearing your ripped Duke sweatshirt and no socks. You are surprised that the dining room doesn't throw you out.

After the candles are lit, your father puts your present on the table between you. It is wrapped in blue and is pliable. Too pliable to be a box. You open it quickly. A book. A book of essays about California.

You love California, he says.

You aren't good at hiding your disappointment.

Little do you know that it will become your favorite book — your favorite possession, really — one that you will carry to college and graduate school and a second graduate school and five different cities and nine different apartments. One that you can recite by memory if someone asks, or even if they don't.

Little do you know that later that very night, you will begin reading this book of essays in your bed, by flashlight, and have one of your first thoughts — as clear and polished as your mom's dining room — that if you could ever create something half as good as this book, you would be a happy person. It will come right before you go to sleep, and so you'll almost miss it. But it is too sure of itself. Bumped against your absolutely unsure thirteen-year-old self. This is what you want your life to become.

Night Four

You pretend not to hear your mother calling. Even though. You don't care that you are keeping her waiting, your entire family waiting   your parents and brother and aunts and uncles and cousins. Everyone in the kitchen together, in from their various towns and cities for this holiday. Everyone waiting for you to light the candles, so they can begin the type of southern feast only your mom is capable of producing: candied apples and roasted turkey, spiced cashews, spinach salad with walnuts, cream-cheese brownie pie.

Not that you care. You are almost seventeen years old, and you are lying on your fluffy white pillows, telephone pasted to your ear, running your fingers through your hair, feeling all grown up in the way you often feel at almost-seventeen: when you are still certain of things, when you still get to be this certain.

On the other end of the phone, Christopher. Your first real boyfriend. You are certain of him. Even though he is too tall and sad and says things that are like warning signs from after-school specials. *Only I'll ever love you this much.* It doesn't matter. You believe him. He is your entire world.

And now he is telling you something important. Something too important for you to hang up, for now, and join your family in the kitchen. Something about a doughnut, you think.

Your mother calls your name again. In another minute, she will either give up or come to your bedroom to get you. She will look at you with disappointment in her eyes.

You hold your hair in your hands, and wait for it.

Night Five

A dorm room. Chilly, dry. You have put several posters on the wall, including one that says LIVE JUICY. Are you living juicy? This is a question you will ask yourself far too many times during your freshman year — your strongest indication that you are not living anything close. You get the candles from someone at Hillel (or you think it is someone at Hillel) who is handing them out on the quad and on Locust Walk. He is also handing out copies of the Adam Sandler Chanukah song on cassette. You think the song is funny, still.

You are waiting for the phone to ring. Does it matter who you are waiting for? Sara G. from down the hall, the silent lacrosse player from your silent-movies seminar? The high school (ex-)

boyfriend now in Oregon? (He barely ever calls when he promises to, and barely ever promises to in the first place.)

You strike your first match. You've made it a ritual to light the candles each night — sometimes with Sara G. from down the hall, tonight by yourself. It feels important to light them, even if by yourself. You watch the lights, as if watching a beehive, feeling incredibly aware of their presence — of how shiny they look — and of something else you are afraid to name. Something that, only later, you can call loneliness.

When the phone rings, you won't hear it.

Night Six

This is your last week in London. And you spend tonight the way you spend every other night this week — lamenting the fact that this is your last week in London.

You have gone out and bought a real menorah for the holiday — because you do everything real here. It feels easy to, right to, which you've come to understand has everything to do with starting to feel right within yourself.

But this isn't the beginning of the thing. The beginning comes months earlier, shortly after you arrive in London for a junior year abroad. When you go with your friend Leigh to her grandparents' home in Manchester, England, for Rosh Hashanah. It is your first time in Manchester — and your first time at an Orthodox temple. The two of you sit with the other women upstairs; the men sit downstairs. Many people — though not you — are wearing very big hats. And someone, maybe the temple president, brings up Chanukah. You remember thinking, That is so long from now. It feels so long from now. My whole life can change by then. (And, months later, you aren't wrong — are you? Not in the ways that matter most.)

But just then, you look over at the seventy-year-old woman wearing the craziest hat of them all: black and white, full of feathers and a bright pink bow.

When she catches your stare, she smiles and gives you a wink.

And you wink back, as if it is possible that this, too, is something you can still learn to do.

Night Seven

It is your first winter in western Massachusetts — in the converted schoolhouse you moved to in order to try to become a writer. Is this something someone can become? Sometimes it feels like a fantasy, like another kind of excuse to hold something like a real life at bay. And still, being here is better than the alternative — better than those difficult months after graduation. The constant throbbing in your head at the Internet company each day. You have picked the wrong life.

Today is twelve degrees below zero, and it is only early December. You have four months of this ahead. You trudge down Main Street to the market to buy some candles. On your way home, you see a billboard advertisement for a local real estate agent. The sign shows a colonial house with a red SOLD sticker across the center, and it reads: IS THIS WHAT IT MEANS TO KNOW WHAT YOU NEED?

You don't know what that means.

But you are having friends over for dinner, are planning to cook salmon and couscous for them — and to make a warm chocolate sponge cake — in your kitchen that is shaped like a boat.

Your windows are twelve feet wide and you have the menorah all set up, all ready to sit in the window closest to your desk, which you keep slightly ajar. You have Joni Mitchell playing in the background, and the food simmering on the stove, and you say the prayer for the seventh night.

Twenty minutes later your doorbell rings, and you race to answer it. And something happens in that moment — you racing, the wind blowing against the windowpane — and for a second, it looks like the menorah is going to tilt, fall in slow motion, right to the floor. Spill all over the carpet, burn the wall on its way down.

You don't consider yourself very religious, but this — you

know — cannot be a good sign. Only then, at the last second — when you realize you can't do anything to stop it — the menorah rights itself.

And this does feel like a sign of something. But maybe it is something simpler than what you are looking for then — which has to do with answering the question on the sign you saw that day. Maybe it has something to do with learning to close the windows tightly in bad weather.

Night Eight

Home again. You recently moved back to New York, recently moved into an apartment four blocks away from where you lived the first time you lived here. It is a quieter apartment — a quieter life, for you — and this time the city doesn't feel wrong, or scary.

And, tonight, you get on the 6:03 train to Westchester, headed to your childhood home, and go to see your parents for the holiday. It is a last-minute trip — and you make it at the last minute; you are out of breath on the train — and close your eyes, trying to catch it.

It has been a long day, and tomorrow will be that way too. But, still, you want to go home tonight. You can see how the whole evening will go — even with your eyes closed, even though you are waiting for it to happen. You will take a nap in your childhood bedroom and drink too much wine at dinner — and then have too much coffee and cake after dinner — and you will look around your family's table, where there are no wrapped gifts waiting this time but where you are reminded of your real gifts: a family who you get to come home to, who have seen you through all these nights, a life you like getting back to.

You are reminded of your real gifts: a family who you get to come home to.

And, after dinner, after loading up on their toilet paper and fresh apples and AA batteries (the things you apparently cannot find in New York City), you will get a ride back to the train station from you dad. You will get ready to go back to your new home. Your second one, the one you are beginning to make for yourself.

But as your dad pulls out of the driveway, you will have a moment in which you remember all the nights that came before. Maybe it will come out of nowhere, or maybe it will happen only after you catch sight of it. The Chanukah lights in the window — shining, like eight simple stories — in the night sky.

ABOUT THE EDITOR

EMILY FRANKLIN is the author of two novels, *The Girls' Almanac* and *Liner Notes,* as well as the critically acclaimed fiction series *The Principles of Love.* She is the editor of *It's a Wonderful Lie: 26 Truths About Life in Your Twenties* and the coeditor of *Before: Short Stories About Pregnancy from Our Top Writers.* Her work has appeared in the *Boston Globe* and the *Mississippi Review* as well as in *Some Kind of Wonderful: Contemporary Writers on the Films of John Hughes* and *When I Was a Loser: True Stories of (Barely) Surviving High School by Today's Top Writers.* She lives near Boston with her husband and their young children. Her Web site is www.emilyfranklin.com.

ABOUT THE CONTRIBUTORS

ELISA ALBERT is the author of the short-story collection *How This Night Is Different*. Her fiction and nonfiction have appeared in *Washington Square*, *Pindeldyboz*, *Nextbook*, *Jewcy*, and the anthologies *Body Outlaws* and *The Modern Jewish Girl's Guide to Guilt*. She lives in Brooklyn and teaches creative writing at Columbia University.

STEVE ALMOND is the author of two story collections, *My Life in Heavy Metal* and *The Evil B. B. Chow*, and a nonfiction book, *Candyfreak*. He lives outside Boston.

KAREN E. BENDER is the author of *Like Normal People*, a novel. She is the coeditor of the anthology *Choice*. Her fiction has appeared in magazines including the *New Yorker*, *Granta*, *Zoetrope*, *Ploughshares*, the *Harvard Review* and has been anthologized in *Best American Short Stories*, *Best American Mystery Stories*, and the Pushcart Prize series. She teaches creative writing at the University of North Carolina at Wilmington, where she and her husband, Robert Siegel, spend the greater part of the year listening to their children's Chanukah gift requests.

JOSHUA BRAFF was born and raised in New Jersey. He studied education at New York University and graduated in 1991. In 1997 he received an MFA in creative writing/fiction from Saint Mary's College in Moraga, California. His first novel, *The Unthinkable Thoughts of Jacob Green,* was nominated for a 2005 Quill Award and made the *San Francisco Chronicle* Best Seller List. It was also one of *Booklist*'s top ten first novels for 2004. His work has appeared in a variety of literary journals, magazines, and anthologies. He lives with his wife and their two children in Oakland, California, and is currently working on his second novel.

LAURA DAVE is the author of the novel *London Is the Best City in America.* Her writing has appeared in *Self, Glamour, ESPN: The Magazine,* and the *New York Observer.* To learn how Laura spends the other Jewish holidays, please visit her Web site: www.lauradave.com.

JENNIFER GILMORE is the author of the novel *Golden Country.* Her work has also appeared in magazines, journals, and anthologies, including *Alaska Quarterly Review, Allure, BookForum, Cutbank, Nerve,* the *Stranger,* and *Salon.* She works in publishing and lives in Brooklyn, New York.

JILL KARGMAN cowrote the novels *The Right Address, Wolves in Chic Clothing, Bittersweet Sixteen,* and *Summer Intern.* Her first solo novel, *Momzillas,* is a dark comedy about competitive type A moms on Manhattan's Upper East Side. She has written for magazines including *Vogue, Harper's Bazaar, Teen Vogue, British GQ, Travel + Leisure,* and *Town & Country.* She lives in New York City with her husband and three children.

AMY KLEIN is a journalist and essayist who has worked in Jerusalem, New York, and Los Angeles, where she currently resides. She has written for numerous Jewish publications, including the *Jerusalem Post*, the *Forward*, the *Jewish Journal of Greater Los Angeles*, and *Hadassah* magazine, as well as mainstream newspapers such as the *San Francisco Chronicle*, the *Chicago Sun-Times*, and the *Los Angeles Daily News*. Her essay "True Confessions of a J-date Addict" appeared in the best-selling anthology *The Modern Jewish Girl's Guide to Guilt.* She received her MFA from Antioch University, Los Angeles.

ADAM LANGER is an author, playwright, and journalist. His novels include *Crossing California, The Washington Story,* and the forthcoming *Ellington Boulevard.* He was born Jewish and has been writing since kindergarten but has been a "Jewish writer" for only about three years.

MAMEVE MEDWED (named for two grandmothers, Mamie and Eva) is the author of the novels *Mail, Host Family, The End of an Error, How Elizabeth Barrett Browning Saved My Life,* and the forthcoming *Men and Their Mothers.* Her short stories, essays, and book reviews have appeared in, among other publications, *Yankee, Redbook, Playgirl,* the *Boston Globe, Ascent,* the *Missouri Review,* the *Washington Post, Confrontation,* and *Newsday.* Born in Bangor, Maine, she lives in Cambridge, Massachusetts.

TOVA MIRVIS is the author of two novels, *The Ladies Auxiliary,* published in 1999, and *The Outside World,* published in 2004. Her essays and fiction have appeared in various anthologies and in newspapers such as the *Forward* and the *New York Times Book Review*. She has an MFA in fiction writing from the Columbia School of the Arts and lives in Newton, Massachusetts, with her husband and their two children.

JOSHUA NEUMAN is the publisher of *Heeb* magazine. A graduate of Brown University and the Harvard Divinity School, he has taught undergraduate courses in the philosophy of religion at New York University, written for *Slate*, ESPN, and Comedy Central, and appeared on VH1, Court TV, and National Public Radio. His first book, *The Big Book of Jewish Conspiracies*, was published in 2005.

ERIC ORNER is a cartoonist and animation artist whose comics and graphic short stories have appeared in *Newsweek*, the *New Republic*, and McSweeney's *Future Dictionary of America*. He has worked on a number of animated features, including a stint as an artist on Disney-Toon Studios' upcoming Tinker Bell movie. A feature film based on Eric's widely syndicated alt-weekly comic strip "The Mostly Unfabulous Social Life of Ethan Green" was released nationally in 2006.

PETER ORNER is the author of *Esther Stories* and the novel *The Second Coming of Mavala Shikongo*. His work has appeared in the *Atlantic Monthly* and the *Paris Review*. Orner is the recipient of the Samuel Goldberg and Sons Foundation Prize for Jewish Fiction, the Rome Prize from the American Academy of Arts and Letters, and a Guggenheim Fellowship. He lives in San Francisco. His middle name is Maxwell.

JOANNA SMITH RAKOFF is the editor of *Nextbook.org*. She has written for *Vogue*, the *New York Times*, and many other publications. She's completing a novel set in Brooklyn.

BEN SCHRANK is the autor of the novels *Miracle Man* and *Consent* and is the publisher of Razorbill, a children's imprint at Penguin. He is at work on a third novel.

EDWARD SCHWARZSCHILD is the author of *Responsible Men,* which was chosen as one of the Best Books of 2005 by the *San Francisco Chronicle* and was a finalist for the Samuel Goldberg and Sons Foundation Prize for Jewish Fiction. Schwarzschild is an associate professor at the University at Albany, SUNY; his book *The Family Diamond* has just been published. You can read more about him and his work at www.thefamilydiamond.com.

ROBERT ANTHONY SIEGEL is the author of the novels *All The Money in the World* and *All Will Be Revealed.* He teaches creative writing at the University of North Carolina at Wilmington, where he lives with his wife, the writer Karen E. Bender, and their two children, Jonah and Maia.

JONATHAN TROPPER is the author of the novels *How to Talk to a Widower, Everything Changes, The Book of Joe,* which was a Book Sense selection, and *Plan B.* He lives with his wife, Elizabeth, and their children in Westchester, New York, where he teaches writing at Manhattanville College. Three of his novels are currently in development as feature films. Jonathan is currently at work on his next novel, and can be contacted through his Web site at www.jonathantropper.com.